PRACTICAL POSITIVE PARENTING

How To Raise Emotionally Intelligent Children Ages 2-7 By Empowering Confidence

HANNAH BROOKS

Practical Positive Parenting

Copyright © 2020 by Hannah Brooks- All rights reserved

No part of this publication may be reproduced, stored in a retrieval system or transmitted in any form or by any means, electronic, mechanical, photocopying, recording, scanning or otherwise, except as permitted under Sections 107 or 108 of the 1976 United States Copyright Act, without the prior written permission of the Publisher.

Limit of Liability/Disclaimer of Warranty: The Publisher and the author make no representations or warranties with respect to the accuracy or completeness of the contents of this work and specifically disclaim all warranties, including without limitation warranties of fitness for a particular purpose. No warranty may be created or extended by sales or promotional materials. The advice and strategies contained herein may not be suitable for every situation. This work is sold with the understanding that the Publisher is not engaged in rendering medical, legal, or other professional advice or services. If professional assistance is required, the services of a competent professional person should be sought. Neither the Publisher nor the author shall be liable for damages arising herefrom. The fact that an individual, organization or website is referred to in this work as a citation and/or potential source of further information does not mean that the author or the Publisher endorses the information the individual, organization or website may provide or recommendations they/it may make. Further, readers should be aware that Internet websites listed in this work may have changed or disappeared between when this work was written and when it is read.

FREE BONUS – 40 SCREEN FREE ACTIVITIES

Practical Positive Parenting

It can be tough keeping your kids occupied indoors and not relying on TV. This is why I've prepared a Free book of the 40 Best Screen Free Activities Your children will love. Activities include doughs, goos, imaginative play in dragon and insect worlds, finger painting, bubbles and much more.

You can get all the necessary ingredients easily at the supermarket. Hours of fun, growth and development await!

Use the link below or scan the QR code to get your Free download instantly!

https://bit.ly/327uEgY

Practical Positive Parenting

CONTENTS

INTRODUCTION 9

THE POSITIVE PARENT 15

WHAT KIND OF PARENT ARE YOU? 17

WHAT IS POSITIVE PARENTING? 25

WHY PRACTICE POSITIVE PARENTING? 35

THE 5 STEPS OF POSITIVE PARENTING 43

STEP #1: IDENTIFY YOUR PARENTAL GOALS 45

STEP #2: SET HEALTHY BOUNDARIES 55

STEP #3: PROVIDE WARMTH & STRUCTURE 62

STEP #4: UNDERSTAND HOW CHILDREN THINK & FEEL ... 73

STEP #5: APPLYING DISCIPLINE IN THE REAL WORLD 83

THE 10 COMMANDMENTS TO PARENT BY 101

AGES 2-4: THE TEN COMMANDMENTS FOR DISCIPLINING TODDLERS 103

AGES 5-7: THE TEN COMMANDMENTS FOR DISCIPLINING OLDER CHILDREN 121

CONCLUSION: YOU'RE ON YOUR WAY 139

viii

INTRODUCTION

Exercise, detox, yoga, meditation, eating well…as an adult, you know how to take care of your body. You know how intention and mindfulness can create the most meaningful, significant moments out of daily routine. You know how being proactive with your health and mental well-being pays dividends.

Why would it be any different with parenting?

Parenting is the great unknown. No one is born knowing how to parent, nor is it a skill normally acquired growing up. Parenting also has the greatest of consequences. The stakes are high—a little person's whole life is riding on your abilities.

How will you parent your child?

How will you know the best way to parent your child?

The good news is it's never too late to be a better parent. You can start today!

Practical Positive Parenting

This quote by author Marisa de los Santos really hits home:

> *"No one is ever quite ready; everyone is always caught off guard. Parenthood chooses you. And you open your eyes, look at what you've got, say "Oh, my gosh," and recognize that of all the balls there ever were, this is the one you should not drop. It's not a question of choice."*

Perhaps that is why we can never seem to get enough parenting advice. That is why so many people hit a mental block when it comes to parenting.

The quantity of advice out there is enough to overwhelm anyone. One expert says to reason with your child; another expert claims that leads to a spoiled rotten child. Should you be using spankings, distraction, timeouts, or bribes to get your child to behave?

With so many choices and even more expert advice, it's perfectly understandable why parents feel flummoxed, worried, and guilty. But as a parent, what you cannot afford to lose are two things: your confidence and your temper.

Take a Deep Breath. You've Got This

This book is about quieting the noise of all those experts.

It turns out that the same principles of positive, proactive caretaking that you apply to your own life can be applied to child-rearing as well. This book will teach you how to approach parenting from a positive mindset, with a focus on strengths instead of weaknesses.

This book will help you to own parenting, and to bring in some of the same mindful, positive techniques that are proven to get results in any area of life. With just five minutes a day, you can work your way through these pages, learning a little each day to apply in your daily parenting challenges.

Practical Positive Parenting

In the pages of this book, you'll learn about the ins and outs of the philosophy of positive parenting. We'll walk through steps that will allow you to integrate the positive parenting philosophy with your own personal parenting quirks and preferences. You'll learn how important healthy boundaries are, and how to satisfy your child's very real craving for boundaries put in place by an adult.

Proven Path to Parenting

Positive parenting and healthy boundaries are not the fad-diet equivalent of raising children. They are not the artificial sweeteners version of it, either. They are the basic building blocks to parenting, the behavioral version of getting your recommended fruits and veggies.

Hundreds of thousands of families have found positive parenting techniques to be useful in solving their child-rearing issues. Thousands have gone before, walking the road of mindful parenting and investing time and effort into their parenting skills.

You can trust the tenets outlined in the bookwork, and that they will make your family dynamic a healthy one. I am passionate about parenting and have raised three children of my own using these very techniques. In my work as a caregiver and nurse, I have seen so many examples of people who have tested these routes to raising and disciplining children, and it speaks for itself.

What Positive Parenting Can Do

Mindful, positive parenting and setting healthy boundaries for your children has a lengthy list of lifelong benefits. Every little bit of progress you make, every argument that is diffused or understanding glance you share with your child, will contribute to the end goal of a child who knows how to express their emotions in a healthy way and respect the emotions of those around them.

By reading and putting into place the tenets set out in this book, you will ensure that your parenting style promotes confidence in your children. Positive parenting is proven to provide children with the tools they need to make good choices, a lasting gift that will serve them as they go out into the real world later on. In the meantime, you can be sure that their relationships with you and their other caregivers will see vast improvements.

This is not a book that comes with a magic wand. This is a book that teaches you how to lay the foundation for a daily practice. Much like yoga, you have to start somewhere and build. No miracles happen overnight, but with a steady hand and consistent application, you can rest assured you are doing the best for your child. You will be able to sit back and watch your child believe in themselves and their future, with empowerment and confidence.

In This Book

In this book, you'll find an in-depth explanation of positive parenting. Read the breakdown of healthy boundaries. What does that mean for you and your child? I outline it here, so that you will be able to implement them in your daily life.

You will find tons of tips you can apply in real time, even in the most tense or difficult situations with your child.

But above all, in this book you will find hints on being proactive with your child. Putting in the time, expressing the love you feel, and making your child feel secure will yield dividends that sheer punishment and discipline never will. You will read about the neuroplasticity of your child's brain, and how you are quite literally shaping it with your daily actions. Toward the end of the book, I break down tips for disciplining your child within the framework of positive parenting. Of course, any parent will tell you that the difference between parenting a child under five and an elementary-school-age child is vast. That's why I've broken discipline tips up into two ages, so you can find which ones apply to your child.

Practical Positive Parenting

Get Started

This book is guaranteed to give you more confidence as a parent. And once you begin to parent with an authoritative air of confidence, your child will respond with greater respect and understanding—naturally. Children are all over the spectrum, of course, but by combining the precepts outlined in this book with your natural parental intuition and knowledge of your child, you'll take the effectiveness of your parenting to the next level.

The information in it is backed by science. Studies have shown that as parents, we have an active role in shaping our children's brains. Parents who consistently use warm, responsive parenting techniques create pathways in their children's brains that are used later in life for emotional intelligence.

Don't wait to read this book—childhood is short, and needless parental suffering shouldn't last any longer than absolutely necessary!

The parenting philosophy and tips that you are about to read have proven results. The chapters of this book will make you feel more in control of your parenting style and help create a positive atmosphere around your home.

Practical Positive Parenting

SECTION ONE

~

THE POSITIVE PARENT

"Children have never been very good at listening to their elders, but they have never failed to imitate them."

— *James Baldwin*

Practical Positive Parenting

~ 1 ~

WHAT KIND OF PARENT ARE YOU?

Ah, parenthood. That fantastical stage of life in which adults go overnight from being someone's child to being an authority on raising one. From being a single solitary person to being the guardian of another. From being able to sit back in the evening and read a book with a glass of wine to trying desperately to parse the meaning in the varying nocturnal cries of a little one.

It's impossible to know what kind of parent you will be until the moment of parenting arrives. An expert, if they hooked you up to some diagnostics for a few tests or asked you about your parents, might be able to discern some of your tendencies. But the mark our own parents leave on us isn't the crystal ball that you might think. There are many more factors that determine the type of parent you are or will become.

And understanding who you are as a parent is one of the keys to unlocking potential magic in the relationship you have with your child.

Practical Positive Parenting

The Four Types of Parent

Parenting is one of the most widely studied and analyzed aspects of family therapy. Years of studies and tons of paper have been devoted to understanding how I myself parent. Four major styles of parenting have been widely recognized: permissive, authoritarian, authoritative, and hands-off. Authoritarian parents are strict disciplinarians, while permissive parents are the opposite, allowing their children to get away with everything. Hands-off parents stay out of their children's way, while the authoritative parent is reasonable, nurturing, and sets clear expectations for their children. Most experts in child development agree that the authoritative parenting style is the most beneficial, resulting in children who are emotionally and academically strong and stable.

Authoritative parenting may sound intimidating, but it's actually the basis of positive parenting. Authoritative parents put a lot of effort into a positive relationship with their child, stepping in to offer explanations and enforce rules when necessary, but always taking their child's feelings into consideration.

Beyond the styles of parenting, there are the styles of parent, as a person. Dr. John Gottman is one of the preeminent thinkers in the world of marriage and family therapy. Recognized by industry reviews as one of the most influential therapists of the past decades, he has created a breakdown of different types of parents that is widely accepted today.[i]

Research shows that emotional awareness is even more important than IQ as a predictor of success in life. In other words, emotion is a decisive factor both in our ability to be parents and in our child's to be successful. The four different types of parent all deal differently with their children and their emotions. Read through the following lists of characteristics and put a check mark by any you identify with.

Parent #1:

- You believe the passing of time will resolve your child's problems
- You tend to disengage from or skip over your child's feelings

Practical Positive Parenting

- When your child has negative emotions, you wish they would just be over quickly
- Sometimes you treat your child's feelings as unimportant
- You think it helps to show your child their feelings aren't a big deal

Parent #2:

- You don't believe in being negative; it's just a waste of time
- The best way to survive is to be emotionally tough. Showing too many emotions makes you weak
- Sometimes you judge and criticize your child for expressing emotions
- You encourage your child to conform to good behavior standards
- Negative emotions are bad and should be kept under control

Parent #3:

- You don't believe in limits
- You think there's not much you can do about negative emotions, so you may as well let them run their course
- However your child expresses their emotion is okay with you
- You don't often help your child solve their problems
- You don't offer much guidance on behavior

Parent #4:

- You are extremely aware of your own emotions and value them
- You would never make fun of your child's negative feelings
- You try not to tell your child how they should feel
- You believe negative emotions can be a teaching moment
- You believe negative emotions can be an opportunity to grow closer
- You like to use words and affection to soothe your child
- You believe it is your job to teach your child how to express emotions in an acceptable manner

Which of the parents' attributes did you identify with the most? Count your checks and see which parent you may be. Read on to find out more about these different types of parents.

Parent #1: The Dismissing Parent

Dismissing Parents are just what they sound like: dismissive of their children's emotions. Don't misunderstand—these parents care deeply for their child and the tendency to dismiss or avoid emotions could be a misguided attempt to prevent their children from feeling negative emotions. The downside? A Dismissing Parent misses many opportunities for emotional connection.

How your child is affected: Your child may get the feeling that their emotions are inappropriate and invalid. This means that they are often unable to regulate their emotions which can be accompanied by a sense there is something wrong with them because of how they feel. They may have difficulty regulating their own emotions.

Parent #2: The Disapproving Parent

The Disapproving Parent has a bit of dismissive behavior, but with a negative edge. For a Disapproving Parent, expressing emotion is considered weak. They focus more on the bad behavior than the negative emotion that may have given rise to that behavior. They often are guilty of suppressing their own emotions, as well.

How your child is affected: Your child has a very similar experience to that of the Dismissing Parent.

Parent #3: The Laissez-Faire Parent

Laissez-faire parents have a loose approach to emotional coaching. Their children may grow up thinking all emotions are accepted no matter what behavior accompanies them. Laissez-faire parents want to give their child every opportunity to be happy, and they do so by leaving a lot of space. Ironically, the lack of guidance inhibits the child's emotional growth.

Practical Positive Parenting

How your child is affected: Your child may not learn to control their emotions. This can express outwardly in having trouble concentrating, forming friendships, and getting along with other kids.

Parent #4: The Emotion Coach

On the surface, Emotion Coaches may seem similar to Laissez-Faire parents, as both allow their children to feel their emotions freely. This parent values all feelings, but not all behavior. They have a strong grasp of their own emotions, which helps them understand those of their child. Emotion Coaches help guide and channel these feelings, aiding their children in recognizing them and then finding a way to express them. This style of parenting takes time and practice but is worth it for the well-adapted people it creates.

How your child is affected: Your child will likely learn to control their emotions and use them to solve their problems. They have self-confidence and are good learners. They also have innate trust in their own feelings.

Which parent are you? Perhaps you found that you identified with more than one. That's natural, too, as parenting styles are greatly influenced by how you were parented, but also a factor of adult decisions and things that have happened in your adult life.

If you find yourself identifying with a parent style that you don't necessarily want to, don't worry. Being a better parent is within your grasp, and the first step is a bit of self-examination.

Practical Positive Parenting

Change is Possible

Now for some good news.

Change is possible! No parent, or person for that matter, is obliged to stay the same. When you gain self-awareness, you take the first step toward change. That is what we will be working toward in the rest of this book: making you a parent that is deeply connected to your child. Creating an atmosphere in which your child feels that connection, thereby often improving behavior before any discipline is even needed or meted out.

This book will provide you with the knowledge that you need to take action. Consistency in taking small steps and putting these strategies into action will eventually shape a new you and a new relationship with your child.

What Your Child Needs from You

All of this self-reflection and change is, fundamentally, for your child. Yes, you may want to save face in the supermarket when your toddler is throwing a tantrum. But as parents, most of us have our child's best interests in the deepest part of our heart. And rightly so—your child is a little person who is very, very dependent on you.

What exactly do our children need from us? Of course, they need a place to sleep that is secure and comfortable. They need shelter. They also need food and clothing. However, it is important to stop and remember that being a parent is so much more than providing these basics. What do you think you offer your child beyond taking care of their physical needs? Take a moment to reflect on that. Is it love? Is it a big hug? Is it gifts? Is it excitement? Is it words of wisdom?

These emotional and mental needs can vary from child to child, but there are basic ones that all children have.

Self-Esteem

Children need to feel good about themselves, and a lot of that development is in the hands of the parents when they are young. A child whose self-esteem has been cultivated is more likely to try hard, cope with mistakes, and do better in school and in relationships. Poor self-esteem can have lasting effects, such as feeling unsure of oneself and limiting participation for fear of not being good enough. Parents can help instill self-esteem by avoiding harsh criticism, by dishing out the appropriate amount of praise when the child does something good, and by helping the child learn.

Security and Safety

Children need a feeling of safety and a secure environment from us. This enables them to feel free to grow, test boundaries, and explore. A child who does not feel safe and secure will be riddled with fear and anxiety. Ways to instill the feeling of safety and security include setting boundaries, being there when your child needs you, remaining calm in the face of adversity, and more.

Relationship Skills Model

Children need to see positive relationships to be able to emulate them later. Modeling the right attitude is important. You can make a difference in your child's future healthy relationship choices. They will look to you to learn about how they should act in relationships, so it's up to you to model things like conflict resolution, communication, and the ability to adjust to stress.

Later in the book, I will talk more about how to provide all of this for your child.

Meanwhile, the most important thing is to remind yourself, always, there is no such thing as a perfect parent. By doing your best as a parent, you have done all you can. It's all right to make mistakes. You will never be perfect. By picking up this book, you have already shown that you are a caring, loving parent. You can do it!

Practical Positive Parenting

~ 2 ~

WHAT IS POSITIVE PARENTING?

People say parenting is more art than science.

That may be true on a day-to-day basis, as parents decide the nuances of how to deal with each beautifully unique child. However, science sheds important light on how we parent, why we parent that way, and what effect a parent can have on their child. So, let's explore a bit of the background of parenting—the psychology.

Positive Psychology

To understand the different styles of parenting, it helps to start at the root. And the root of positive parenting is in its father branch, positive psychology.

Positive psychology is the scientific study of what makes life worth living. Truly! But what does that really mean?

Practical Positive Parenting

According to the Positive Psychology Center, positive psychology is "the scientific study of the strengths that enable individuals and communities to thrive. The field is founded on the belief that people want to lead meaningful and fulfilling lives, to cultivate what is best within themselves, and to enhance their experiences of love, work, and play." [ii]

A psychologist who practices positive psychology will place emphasis on their patients' strengths, not their weaknesses. They will focus on perfecting skills and fortifying the good more than fixing the bad. The so-called father of positive psychology, Martin Seligman, was the president of the American Psychological Association. At the turn of the twenty-first century, he began to theorize that psychology should move away from the last half century of psychopathology and focus more on the positive side of life. He felt building human strengths was a good complement to the traditional psychologist role of healing damage. [iii]

To put it simply, positive psychology shines the light on the sources of psychological wellness: positive emotions, experiences, environments, and human strength.

To sum it up, positive psychology has the following goals:

- Engage well with others
- Rise to the challenges in life despite any setbacks
- Help others, not just yourself, to find lasting meaning and satisfaction
- Find fulfillment through things like productivity and inventiveness

Positive psychology looks a lot like today's mindfulness movement. If you have ever kept a gratitude journal or done a meditation to ground you in the moment, you've put positive psychology into practice. What you will find truly useful, however, is how the tenets of positive psychology look when applied to parenting.

CALL TO ACTION!

One morning or evening when you have a bit of time to yourself, practice a bit of positive psychology. Think of someone who has done something for you that you are grateful for. What was it? How did it make you feel? Take note of these things, either in your journal, on the Notes app of your phone, or even in a letter. The next time you see or speak with this person, express your gratitude toward them, sharing what you realized as you did the exercise above. Alternately, mail that letter. Reflect on how you feel after you do this, and how long this feeling lasts.

Practical Positive Parenting

So, What is Positive Parenting?

"You need to be harder on her."

"Tough love is the best policy."

"All that touchy-feely stuff is just going to ruin him."

Perhaps, in an effort to employ different techniques with your children, you have heard some of these phrases. Not from your child, but from your parents, your relatives, or even your partner. Guess what? It's not their fault. Old habits die hard, as do old customs and psychological theories. Most likely, they are repeating the parenting mantras that they were taught and put into use, and not necessarily because they work or even because they like them. They are likely repeating them to you merely because they need to feel justified in their own personal parenting style.

If you're reading this book, the chance is you do not come with this kind of baggage, or if you do, you are interested in swapping it for some brand-new suitcases.

I strongly believe that positive parenting is the best theory we can possibly apply to our child-rearing techniques nowadays.

So what is positive parenting?

Positive parenting can be defined as "the continual relationship of a parent(s) and a child or children that includes caring, teaching, leading, communicating, and providing for the needs of a child consistently and unconditionally."[iv]

What does that mean, exactly?

Positive parenting is all about guiding, leading by example, teaching discipline in a way that gives the child the power and motivation to follow rules, allowing your child to be themselves, yet all the while supporting a mutually respectful parent-child relationship.

Positive parenting, by virtue of its positive psychology roots, is in fact a more proactive way of being a parent. Instead of superimposing tough discipline on a situation, you are working with your child on a daily basis to proactively provide them with the tools they need and crave to behave. You will react, of course, if the boundaries that positive parents set are broken. However, the majority of a parent's energy in positive parenting is spent taking proactive steps to strategically position their child for success.

Positive psychology rests on a few basic ideas that are helpful to be aware of:

#1 Children Primarily Desire to Belong

After their material needs have been met (clothing, shelter, food), children yearn to feel a sense of belonging and importance. They need to feel wanted, part of a tribe. In the child's world, that usually means being a part of a family. This is why big changes, like divorce or a new brother or sister, can throw off their behavior. They need to feel needed, to know that they have an important part in their family and have the capacity to act in that world. **Parents must give their children positive ways to show their power and autonomy;** if they don't, they will show it in negative ways, by talking back or entering into a power struggle.

#2 All Behavior Has A Meaning

Children's behavior always has a meaning, something your child is trying to tell you. Look at behavior as a symptom, not a problem, and you can get to the bottom of each issue and perhaps even correct it.

#3 A Child Who Misbehaves Needs Something

This principle dates back to the founding of parenting psychology: a child who misbehaves is not bad, mean, or uncontrollable. They are simply not having their needs met. Which needs? The need to belong and feel important. This is the way a child knows how to communicate. As parents, we should try to deal with the root of the problem.

Practical Positive Parenting

Where Did Positive Parenting Come From?

Positive parenting has a long history, dating back to the beginning of the twentieth century. Believe it or not, until a hundred years ago, the idea that a parent could even really *prepare* for parenthood didn't exist in the United States. Dr. Alfred Adler introduced this idea to a skeptical audience in the 1920s. However, other experts followed and the theory blossomed. Jane Nelsen wrote *Positive Discipline* in 1981, and it became a classic that is still in print today. The idea developed into a full-blown method, going on to inspire variations and different varieties, such as the Positive Parenting Program developed in Australia in 2001.

Parenting With Emotions

Let's go back to the parenting quiz from Chapter 1. What type of parent were you? The Gottman Institute, where these divisions were identified, puts forth the Emotion Coach as the parent to emulate. What if you weren't identified as an Emotion Coach? Does that mean you have to throw out your parenting tactics and trade them for a new set of techniques? Well…if you're playing tennis and someone tells you if you grip the racket a tiny bit higher you'll get more power on your swing, do you have to go back to not knowing the difference between a forehand and a backhand? Not at all. Our journey as parents should be rich, fruitful, and continuous. This means finding things that complement your beliefs and adding them to your parental repertoire.

What Dr. Gottman has done is compile loads of research on children, during an age when the serious experts spoke more about misbehavior management than anything else. What percentage of the time are our children misbehaving, really? It may feel like most of the time, but in reality, there are many more moments when things are calm, or even good. Gottman fixated on this and started detailed lab studies of children and parents. Here are the tenets of the Emotion Coach parent that he created after analyzing his studies.

Be Aware of Your Child's Emotion

Tune in. Set your cell phone facedown and tune in to what your child is doing, saying, and feeling. This is a very powerful exercise, and you may be surprised at how it feels. You might even realize that it's something that you don't normally do as fully as you would like to.

Recognize your child's expression of emotion as a teaching moment

Your child, when they express emotion, is sharing with you. Repeat that thought to yourself. Your child wants to open themselves up to you, to show you a piece of their heart. This moment is a great one to put yourself on their wavelength and meet them halfway with some words of parental wisdom. What does this look like? Less like giving advice and more like asking questions or telling stories, actually!

Listen with Empathy and Validate Your Child's Feelings

Our children are expert expression readers. They are more in tune with us and our emotions oftentimes than we are ourselves. So they can tell when you are listening. Be sure to show them they have your attention, which will make them feel that you are empathizing with them. Validate their feelings by, for example, repeating them back to show you've heard and that they are worthy of being spoken.

Help Your Child Learn to Label Their Emotions with Words

Sometimes, especially with younger children, it will be difficult for them to put their feelings into words. They simply don't yet have the complex vocabulary required to express the wide range of emotions they may be feeling. That's where you can step in, leading by example and helping them to put words to their feelings.

Practical Positive Parenting

Set Limits When You Are Helping Your Child to Solve Problems, or Deal with Upsetting Situations Appropriately[v]

We will talk more about this in future chapters, but letting your child know about appropriate and inappropriate ways of dealing with their situation gives them the power to be creative within those limits. Having limits is a comforting feeling when you are out of your comfort zone, and it challenges them to push their problem-solving skills.

As you can see, all of these tenets require us to forget our parental agenda and tune in to the present moment. That is the gift of the Emotion Coach parent, and it's a gift that with a bit of practice any of us can come to possess. The best part? They will help you to connect more closely with your child.

> CALL TO ACTION!
>
> Next time you hear your child expressing a negative emotion, walk through the tenets. Pay special attention to listening with empathy, validating your child's feelings, and helping your child to label their feelings. Stick with them throughout the process. You may be surprised at the result!

Most importantly, emotion coaching puts the tools into the hands of your children. Naysayers or nagging self-doubt may tell you that you are feeding the situation or raising a drama queen. That is simply not true. What you are doing when you coach your child's emotions is teaching them a few very important things:

- **Emotions are confusing.** They can be hard to pin down for a young one, and emotion coaching lets kids know that is all right. It also helps them to notice their feelings, so they are prompted to use words instead of force.
- **Emotions are okay.** They are not dangerous, although they can be overwhelming. But just staring them in the face teaches a child not to fear them.

Practical Positive Parenting

- **Emotions can be managed.** When you give them a voice, emotions remain under control. This gives you and your child power to manage difficult emotions, such as anger.

The Steps

As you can see from this chapter, positive parenting and emotional coaching go hand in hand. There are steps to the process, which we will be looking at one by one in the upcoming chapters. The steps are the following:

- Reflect & Identify Your Goals as a Parent
- Lay the Foundation by Setting Healthy Boundaries
- Create an Atmosphere of Warmth and Structure
- Listen, Hear, Understand
- React Appropriately, aka Discipline in the Real World

Read on to learn more about these steps in the following chapters. They will give you the road map to discipline your children with love, while at the same time, helping your children to develop emotional intelligence.

Just think, you are giving your child the gift of a lifetime: the ability to work through conflict in relationships and a natural capacity for regulating their emotions. As you put these steps into action, watch as your child becomes more empathetic with you and with their siblings. I promise!

Practical Positive Parenting

~ 3 ~

WHY PRACTICE POSITIVE PARENTING?

"The way we talk to our children becomes their inner voice."

— *Peggy O'Mara*

There are a lot of styles of parenting. So why positive parenting? It stands to reason that, before you edit and reshape your parenting policies, you'd want to know why you should. In this chapter, we'll talk about the effects that positive parenting has. Positive parenting has benefits that are backed by scientific studies—we'll talk about those. It also has more intangible or abstract positive effects. Read on to find out why positive parenting is worth trying.

Practical Positive Parenting

The Proactive Solution

One of the biggest differences between positive parenting and other parenting styles or solutions is that positive parenting is proactive. Positive parenting puts the healthy control in the hands of the parent yet leaves the child space to feel a sense of control and to do their part.

Think about it.

Life is hectic, and our family lives can be even more so.

Positive parenting provides parents with strategic tools, so that your parenting technique doesn't consist solely of putting out fires. This prevents important things, like quality time with your child, from being overlooked or pushed to the side.

Do you want to be that parent running after a toddler through the aisles of a supermarket, shouting "Don't do that or I'll punish you!"? Or would you rather be the one who is in tune with their child, calmly able to redirect or help their toddler express their feelings pre-meltdown?

Positive parenting allows you to stop reacting and instead focus on responding with your whole attention and whole heart to your children.

Training the Brain

Our children are born sweet, cuddly, and helpless. We know instinctively they need us to take care of them. Science shows us exactly why, and it's fascinating.

Neuroscience has a lot to say about early brain development. The experiences we give our children complement the genetic factors that have already formed them. Our children's brains are magical things, sitting there like sponges waiting to be filled. The talk-and-respond you automatically do with your tiny baby is actually one of the most important early experiences they can have for their brain. This social interaction and mirroring of baby's actions, expressions and speech effectively wires the brain to be able to proceed on a normal growth pattern.

Practical Positive Parenting

Your baby's brain is being shaped in these first few years, and every time you soothe them, their brain builds a neural pathway to soothe. By soothing your baby, you help them be able to eventually soothe themselves.

Younger children's brains continue developing through their teen years. During these years, it is vital for us to give our children stimulation, both academic and artistic. They need physical, social and emotional experiences to continue positive brain development.

The word for this magic process is **neuroplasticity.** It is the brain's ability to reorganize itself in response to changes in situations and environment. Within the brain, this basically looks like new neural connections routed and re-routed by neurons in the brain.

Top researchers came together to study this concept in children, to remarkable results.

They studied how the brain structure changed in children who received positive parenting, parents with a warm, consistent parenting style. They also contrasted it with children whose parents used a negative, aggressive style to parent.

The findings showed that, during childhood and teenage years, the human brain has a heightened sensitivity and ability to change. The researchers found that positive parenting, especially by the mother, correlate with real, physical changes in several parts of the brain: the striatum, which is the brain's reward system; the amygdala, which helps us interpret emotion and feeling; and the brain's orbitofrontal and anterior cingulate cortex, which is what we activate when we make decisions and use self-control. Children who had a more negative upbringing had difficulty with these skills and tended to keep all their feelings inside.

Get this—other studies have shown that strong parental bonds and relationships have a lasting effect on cortisol levels in the brain. Cortisol is the stress hormone, and our bodies need it to boost energy, balance stress levels, control our sleep cycles and regulate blood pressure, blood sugar, and inflammation. So, it's pretty important.

Practical Positive Parenting

Positive parenting builds better brain architecture—a structure your child will live with for the rest of their life.

Benefits of positive parenting for your child

The benefits of positive parenting are wide ranging and long lasting. They are also backed up by research and studies—these are not just anecdotal thoughts, they are real and proven. Reading through this list, ask yourself if your child would benefit from any of them.

Confidence

The teaching and leading inherent in positive parenting helps promote children's confidence. A confident child is secure about who they are. They are more likely to take on new challenges and learn from mistakes.

Problem solving

Children whose parents practiced positive parenting have increased problem-solving skills.

Better relationships

Positive communication between child and parent means children will then have better-quality relationships with other adult figures and children their age. They will learn to decipher both verbal and nonverbal cues, a vital part of being a functioning adult.

Self-esteem

Responsive parenting feels warm and gives children a sense of security. They know they have a democratic, fair parent. This, in turn, enhances their self-esteem.

Empowerment

A parenting style that places emphasis on the child's autonomy, as does positive parenting, supports creativity and empowerment.

Optimism

Children who have support from optimistic parents come out with a greater belief in themselves and their future, and increased optimism.

Decreased risky behavior

When parents recognize actions they do approve of, they motivate children to pursue these positive behaviors, thereby decreasing the likelihood of risky behavior.

Responsibility

Boundaries are the magical tool that not only serves to put order in the house, but actually helps children increase their responsibility and accountability levels.

A little bit of effort goes a long way. These benefits have even been shown to mitigate other risk factors for negative behavior, such as being a single parent or being economically disadvantaged. It's nice to know that whatever your situation may be, the power is in your hands as a parent to rear a healthier, better-adapted child.

Isn't that what we all want to hear?

Practical Positive Parenting

Benefits of positive parenting on others

Of course, your children aren't the only ones who benefit when you put positive parenting into practice. A surprising benefactor of these parenting practices hasn't even been born yet: your child's child.

A study from Oregon State University shows that positive parenting definitively affects a child's future parenting style. This study was taken over three generations of families, in which over 200 male children were studied, along with their parents. They met with researchers every year for 24 years, enabling the researchers to really pinpoint how factors from their own childhood affected their parenting style.

The study was important because it showed that, in addition to the generational impact of negative behaviors, positive ones are just as likely to get "passed down." The study went on to explain that it's not really about mimicking behavior; it's more about the negative impact angry, threatening parenting has on a child's adolescence, and how that troubled adolescence goes on to effect their parenting skills.[vi]

In addition to behavioral effects, changes in your child's environment can also lead to gene-plasticity. Epigenetics is the branch of science that studies these changes, in which certain environmental factors result in changes to the way a gene is expressed. Occasionally, these changes remain in the genes and get passed down to children. For example, in one study of a small community in rural Sweden, it was shown that life expectancy was significantly higher in men whose grandfathers experienced a failed crop season before they hit puberty. Something about the starvation in their environment made a change to their genes, and that change passed on through generations.

Just another reason that how you parent really does matter!

Practical Positive Parenting

Benefits of positive parenting for YOU!

As parents, we do anything for our children. When it comes to practicing positive parenting, however, the motivation doesn't have to be 100 percent altruistic.

It's important to point out that positive parenting has benefits for you, too.

Positive parenting gives tools to the parent that will help them navigate parenthood with more calm and cool. While at first it may be difficult to regulate your emotions when your child is misbehaving, after every single time you manage to contain that anger and reflect a calm, positive attitude, it will be easier. And just like that old adage that smiling actually makes you happier, even if you fake it, faking calm will help you actually feel calm, in addition to diffusing a difficult situation.

The emphasis on warm connection within the framework of positive parenting is another aspect that will bring you great benefits in your parent-child relationship. You will see improvement in how you and your child relate to each other. Another benefit of this connection is increased obedience. Children that feel connected to their parents are more likely to follow your guidance, which is vital as they grow bigger, stronger, and closer to being an adult.

If you've ever felt that sense of exhaustion from trying to control or bargain with your child all day, you know how much it takes out of you to be bargaining and disciplining all day long. When the tenets of positive parenting are applied continuously, you will see this feeling ease off and find yourself in more of a coach role, versus a controlling one.

Our goal as parents is to raise human beings whom we ourselves want to spend time with. Humans who treat other humans well. Human evolution as social beings proves that connection is the key to shaping your child's character.

Being respectful to your child and listening to them—major tenets of positive parenting—isn't spoiling them. It is treating your child like a human being. And setting them up for a positive future.

Practical Positive Parenting

SECTION TWO

~

THE 5 STEPS OF POSITIVE PARENTING

"Parenting is the easiest thing in the world to have an opinion about, but the hardest thing in the world to do."

—— *Matt Walsh*

Practical Positive Parenting

~ 4 ~

STEP #1: IDENTIFY YOUR PARENTAL GOALS

Parenting is one of those jobs you just have to do to really know what you are doing. Best-laid plans are the first ones to crumble when pitted against a real-life, meltdown-prone toddler, child or teenager. Whatever you may have thought about how you would parent and what being a parent would be like, you probably had a quick reality check when you brought home your baby!

There is one thing that is certain, however.

Raising a child is both harder and even more joyful and rewarding than you ever imagined.

As I mentioned before, parenting is most definitely an art. However, it can be dissected and broken down in a way that gives us, as parents, the tools to tackle it. A little bit of thought, along with a little bit of training, and a little bit of mindfulness.

Practical Positive Parenting

> **CALL TO ACTION!**
>
> Create your parenting mantra.
>
> What exactly does that mean? A mantra is a short phrase that can be repeated over and over, out loud or mentally. A parenting mantra will remind of your abilities as a parent or, perhaps, inspire you to be better as a parent. By saying it over and over, you cement it in your mind so that in the heat of the moment, it pops into your head and informs your action.
>
> Here are some examples of parenting mantras:
>
> - Stop. Breathe.
> - I am patient.
> - They are not their bad behavior.
> - Give a hug instead.
> - I can let go of this.
>
> Write it down and leave it somewhere visible where you can read it several times a day.

Automatic vs Deliberate Parenting

As I make this call to you to become more mindful with your parenting, starting with goal setting, it's helpful to take a step back. After all, maybe you didn't think to set a parenting mantra, or parenting goals, before reading this book. Why not?

Well, because you are like many other parents.

In his book *1-2-3 Magic,* Thomas Phelan sets out by determining two different types of parenting modes: automatic and deliberate. According to Phelan, "Automatic parenting includes the things you do spontaneously without really thinking (and with no real training), such as picking up and comforting a sobbing two-year-old who has just fallen down." There are many examples of how automatic parenting helps us, relying on our instincts to take care of our children.

However, there are also many examples of how automatic parenting can go wrong. For example, picture your child being frightened by an imaginary sound late at night. They continue to get out of bed, insisting that there is something in their room. It's late, you're tired and you lose your temper with them, shouting for them to go back to bed. That is an example of automatic parenting that can potentially be revised.

The deliberate parenting mode is when our automatic parenting goes through a filter before it reaches our child. The parent in deliberate mode replaces negative actions with ones that they have thought through, deliberately choosing ones that respect their child. Eventually, these deliberate actions become automatic. [vii]

Why set parenting goals?

So why should we set parenting goals?

Goal setting in general is a powerful way to think about what you want from the future. Once you capture your goals, they are there, serving as motivation for you in moments when you lose sight of the finish line. They help you turn your visions into reality.

As we go through the process of becoming a deliberate parent and adapting positive parenting techniques, goal setting is a tool we can use to keep ourselves on track.

After all, as I mentioned earlier, nobody wakes up a perfect parent. It is a learning process, paved with parenting books, experiences from our own lives, and cherry picking from ideas and models we see around us. When we approach parenting with a deliberate, mindful process, using tools like goal setting, we constantly improve how we parent our children. This has an added bonus for you: parenting will seem easier, more natural, and even carefree.

Practical Positive Parenting

If you think about it, whether you mindfully set parenting goals or not, you are acting on short-term goals. You want your child to come in the house, to stop fighting, to look both ways before crossing the road, to put on their jacket. These short-term goals and responses lack both a strategy and a lesson for the child. They are not helping your child to become a great communicator, confident, or good problem solver. Depending on how you administer them, they may even be preventing you from achieving these long-term goals.

By setting long-term parenting goals, you will find yourself spending more quality, stress-free time with your kid. With your goals at hand, you have the ability to turn short-term challenges into strategic opportunities. Your child will learn, over time, to communicate and handle conflict, giving them the long-term confidence to achieve anything. And you'll look back and know you parented to the best of your ability.

Identifying your parental goals

We all walk into this world of parenting with a different set of skills. You will bring a different expertise and strengths to parenting than your partner, your neighbors, or your child's friend's parents. This makes the process of goal setting a very individual one.

- What do you want to improve on?
- Which aspect of your parenting would you like to change?
- Take a moment to reflect on that. If you're feeling stumped or uninspired, ask yourself what the hardest part of parenting is for you.
- Perhaps you would like more patience.
- Maybe you lack one-on-one time with your children.
- Do you feel like all you do is clean up after your family?
- Do your children resist listening to you?
- Do you find yourself yelling more than you'd like?
- Are your kids fighting a lot?
- Perhaps you don't feel comfortable with how much screen time your kids have.
- Maybe you wish for more time to recharge your own batteries.

Practical Positive Parenting

> **CALL TO ACTION!**
> Make a list of things you'd like to improve or fix about your own parenting style and techniques. Don't think too hard, just make as exhaustive a list as you can.

I've spoken with a lot of parents over the years. I've heard the same concerns voiced over and over again. I've identified these oft-repeated goals and distilled them down. Here are some of the most recurring parental goals I've heard from parents over the years. I hope some of them might serve as inspiration as you identify your parental goals.

Be consistent when it comes to rules

Kids are infamous for not following rules. Part of their nature is to want to test the limits. They want to see if we are firm and if our rules are truly hard and fast. Another reason, however, for kids not following rules could be that they just aren't clear enough. Or one day, your child is punished for breaking a rule and the next day your child is not.

If this is a goal for you, here are some concrete actionable steps:

- Define your rules clearly
- Communicate them even more clearly with your children
- Communicate the consequences of breaking the rules
- Explain the consequences to your children
- Follow through on the consequences

Deepen your family connection

In this day and age, this is one I hear all the time. Parents want to know their kids, perhaps more than any other generation before. We, as parents, also yearn for quality time. Getting to the deepest level of your child's thoughts and personality is a magical pursuit.

If this is a goal for you, here are some concrete actionable steps:

- Set aside time for one-on-one with each of your kids
- Use the time before bed to bond
- Make dinner a sacred time where conversation reigns
- Plan a getaway for the whole family

Make family values a cornerstone

Figure out which values your family stands for—for many of us, that would be kindness, respect and compassion. Sometimes these intangible values can be the first to go in a stressful moment or when checking off daily to-do lists. But you can take that time and attention back and encourage your kids to uphold those values.

If this is a goal for you, here are some concrete actionable steps:

- Incorporate being respectful (or whatever your values are) into your list of family rules
- The first person to follow and exemplify this values must be you
- Use books and movies to transmit the values, and talk about them after you read/watch

Practical Positive Parenting

Instill more responsibility in your kids and do less for them

Sometimes our efficiency gets in the way of this goal. Yes, in the short term it is often easier to 'do it yourself.' However, teaching our children independence is a vital part of their upbringing. If you are always doing it all, you are also simultaneously doing your children a disservice.

If this is a goal for you, here are some concrete actionable steps:

- Define a daily chore for your child
- Do harder tasks with children the first few times
- Be very specific when giving jobs to young children
- Be patient with the results—don't "fix" your child's hard work unless it's dangerous

Get your kids to listen to you more often

There's nothing more frustrating than when your children just don't listen. That feeling of powerlessness can make you react in ways you never meant to. So many parents' goal is to just get their kids to listen.

If this is a goal for you, here are some concrete actionable steps:

- Speak clearly and in a neutral or positive tone
- Add a family rule that talks about listening the first time
- Tell them what to do instead of what *not* to do
- Utilize positive reinforcement when they do listen to you

Practical Positive Parenting

Yell less

This is another one of the most popular goals I hear from parents. Yelling just doesn't do anything in the long term. And it is doubly frustrating as an adult, because after a nice yelling session, no matter the outcome, you realize that your child is actually the one in power. The good news is you *can* parent without yelling.

If this is a goal for you, here are some concrete actionable steps:

- Figure out what makes you angry, and find ways to avoid it
- When you feel anger coming on, remove yourself for a "time-out"
- Map out your angry times. You may find they tend to happen around the same time of day, and that will give you a key to solving them
- Calm down before reacting

Have less screen time in your house

Your parents probably didn't have to deal with this issue, but it plagues parents today. Screens are easy and kids love them. They can be educational, but they are also addicting and have unresolved potential health concerns. Screens are convenient, helpful, and fun. And while there are definite advantages to them and moments where we can rely on them, science has shown us time and time again that our kids' generation (and their parents) are becoming quickly addicted.

If this is a goal for you, here are some concrete actionable steps:

- Use technology to combat technology, such as apps that monitor screen time and usage
- Make a rule that's easy to follow, like no screens on weekdays
- Make sure there are alternatives in the house, like books and games

Practical Positive Parenting

> **CALL TO ACTION!**
> Look over your list and make any additions you have thought of.
> Now circle those that are extremely important to you. Try to
> narrow them down to a top 5. With those five, write out the goal
> in a complete sentence in your journal, or somewhere you can
> return to reference it.

In no way are these all the changes or goals that you can make. As I always like to say, parents know best. Curate your own list, and keep it in the back of your mind. You probably won't have the time or the bandwidth to do everything on the list, but if you keep it on the back burner, you will notice that moments start arising for you to take action steps.

You should give yourself a pat on the back for taking the initiative! To help you along the process, in the rest of the chapter you'll find some more tips on setting (and following through on) your goals.

Effective Goal Setting

As you go on to identify your goals as a parent, here are some general tips for setting an effective goal. Remember, you are laying the foundation now upon which the rest of the positive parenting process is built. Take your time and enjoy the process!

- This process is for you and you alone. There are no 'shoulds' and there is no one watching and judging your choices. So make sure you are choosing goals that are consistent with your parenting vision. Choose a goal that feels like it will move you toward who you want to be.

- Get that goal down on paper. Make it big, bold, and into something that resonates with you. Above all, put it somewhere where you will see it and it can serve as a daily reminder. That is the power of goal setting: keeping it in your mind to take tiny steps forward whenever possible.

Practical Positive Parenting

- When talking about or writing your goal, speak as if it is already happening. By saying "I am a strong, patient mom who listens before she speaks," you actually trick your brain into thinking it's true and acting accordingly.

- Be sure to frame your goal without any negative words, like "no," "don't," or "won't." The same concept applies to raising your children, as we will read in future chapters.

- Put a date on it. One of the most effective goal-setting strategies is to give yourself a deadline. Another effective strategy is to place the goal within your current schedule. When will you enact the steps to this goal so that you complete it by your deadline?

After setting these goals, it helps to keep them at the top of your mind.

According to the principles of Dr. Maxwell Maltz's success mechanism, we must integrate these goals into our imagination and our action for them to work. His theories are proponents of the power of imagination, which, used purposefully, can reprogram your doubts and subconscious. According to Dr. Maltz, writing these goals down must be followed by a visualization in which you see the outcome as clearly and as if it were really happening.

Maltz's concepts of visualization are indeed a powerful part of goal setting.

> CALL TO ACTION!
> Take ten minutes to yourself in a quiet place. Close your eyes, and visualize your family interacting when one of your parenting goals is achieved. How does everyone act? What is the atmosphere like? Envision it in the most detailed manner possible, really visualizing the situation.

Once you have identified and visualized your parental goals, you are ready for Step #2: Set Healthy Boundaries.

~ 5 ~

STEP #2: SET HEALTHY BOUNDARIES

You did it. You have your goals in mind, and you're ready to get down to business. Here comes a huge part of laying the foundation for positive parenting. Are you ready?

Keep in mind that by reading this book, you are already achieving something—you are taking steps to improving the way you parent. There will be bumps along the way, but in this chapter you'll learn about how to keep things on track. If positive parenting were running a marathon, in the last chapter we decide we are going to run it, and in this chapter we are setting up our training plan.

What Are Healthy Boundaries?

Healthy boundaries are the law of the land. They define the what-you-can and what-you-can't of your children's lives. They protect both your children and your sanity. They're more complicated than rules, though. Some of these boundaries are hard to put into words. Some of them are hard for children to follow.

Healthy boundaries are the limits you put in place in order to identify the ways your children are allowed to act toward you. Boundaries can be physical, emotional, or even psychological. It can be just as crucial to set these less tangible psychological boundaries as it can be to set the physical ones.

They are necessary for you as a parent, yes, but they are also an important tool in your children's development. A defining part of a healthy boundary is "the other side," as in, what happens when the boundary is crossed. That is why consequences are a vital part of clear boundaries.

But the biggest secret about healthy boundaries?

Your kids crave them.

Why Is Setting Healthy Boundaries Important?

Some things are very logical in the parenting game. Your child is hungry? Feed them. They are crying? Comfort them. Other times, however, the parenting game works counterintuitively. Boundaries are an example of an aspect of parenting that is not quite straightforward.

You see, setting and honoring boundaries is a key element of a healthy relationship with your child. Children crave limits. Most children would never acknowledge this, but as the world stretches infinitely before them, waiting to be explored, it helps comfort them to know that there are limits to that infinity, limits in which they will be safe and sound and accompanied by someone.

These boundaries serve as the framework with which your child sees the world. Explaining these boundaries with warmth and love helps to create a livable world for a child.

Practical Positive Parenting

Another reason setting healthy boundaries is important is because it models a skill that your child will need for the rest of their life. As they grow and form relationships outside the family, there will come a time when they need to be able to set, communicate, and enforce healthy boundaries themselves. By modeling this behavior first, you help your child learn to advocate for themselves and for their needs.

Perhaps you or your partner is hesitant to set boundaries. Some people think that setting boundaries will mean they have to enforce those boundaries with negative discipline. Others think setting a limit will make their child love them less. Ironically, it is completely the opposite.

That pushback we receive when we set boundaries for our children is not them being angry and thinking "how unfair!"—it is actually an impulse on their part. Our children are hard-wired to test boundaries. It may help to think of your child as a scientist, collecting data with every transgression in order to form a hypothesis. It is part of their development, and it is how they answer common questions.

- Do my parents love me?
- Will they care for me?
- Are my parents confident in their leadership?
- Are they on my side or against me?
- Are my own feelings okay?

Being a child is scary sometimes, and healthy boundaries create an environment where children know exactly where they stand, why their behavior is or isn't acceptable, and how they are expected to act. Healthy boundaries create strong individuals with a marked identity and good emotional and mental health.

Boundaries will vary by child, but the important part is to find the middle ground between boundaries that provide security and those that make a child feel overly controlled. Read on to find out about the steps to setting healthy boundaries.

Practical Positive Parenting

The Steps To Setting Healthy Boundaries

As a parent, it is up to you to be the model for healthy boundary setting.

So where do you start?

Get a clear picture

To set healthy boundaries, you must first have a clear picture about what your values and rules are within your family. You need to know yourself and be aware of what you are modeling for your child. What are the most important things to you in your life?

Make a plan

The next step is to make a plan. How will you maintain this boundary in the moment, when your child is potentially screaming and you are about to blow up? You need to find a tool that allows you to be solid and firm regarding the boundary.

Communicate the boundaries

Then comes what is perhaps the most important step: communicating the boundaries to your child. Choose a time when all is calm to communicate the new "rule" to your child. Explain the why and communicate your expectations. During this stage, STAY SIMPLE. Do not go into loads of detail or explain the history behind the boundary. Just state it and give an explanation of why it is important, whether that reason is for safety, because of rules, or because it backs up one of your family values. Encourage children to ask questions at this stage.

Set consequences

The final step is setting the consequences for breaking the boundary. Put some big, verbal emphasis on this part, as it is an essential part in the process. Be strong and sure in the fairness of your boundaries, so that you can say no when it is truly necessary. Make sure the consequences match the crime, however, knowing that you will likely at some point have to use them.

Practical Positive Parenting

Follow through

The step that never ends is the follow-through. Enforcing the boundaries you have put into place is vital. Remember, your child will benefit from these limits as they are consistently and warmly enforced. Let them feel the full impact of a crossed boundary and its consequences. As an important side note, it is key to stay flexible. Your child will grow and certain age-appropriate boundaries may need to be expanded. Consider holding family meetings to help review progress.

And that's it! Consistency, consistency, and consistency will be your best friend. Keep in mind the importance of this task whenever you get discouraged…you are setting up your child for interpersonal and relationship success for the rest of their life by showing them how to set and abide by healthy boundaries with responsibility and kindness.

The Obstacles to Healthy Boundaries

Nobody said this was easy.

If you're anything like me, you may feel unqualified for all this at first. Don't worry! I always say that children actually continue where our parents left off, teaching us and helping us grow into the full-blown adult that we want to be. Remember that if you are trying your best, that will be good enough for your child.

That said, there are some common obstacles people run up against when going through the above boundary-setting process. Read up on them or bookmark this page to return to it later.

You've probably been tossing around a few ideas in your head for healthy boundaries you want to set in your family, or perhaps thinking of the boundaries that already exist which just need to be named.

Lack of teaching

Most of us aren't taught to set boundaries as kids. You may feel like you don't know what you're doing. Don't worry, you'll get the hang of it. The desire to learn and willingness to practice (and to get it wrong) are all it takes.

Practical Positive Parenting

Guilt

If you aren't used to setting boundaries, it may feel unnatural at first. You might even feel guilty. But just be sure to keep telling yourself that it is a necessary step for your mental health. By setting them now, you are teaching your child that it is all right, even vital, to do so.

Pressure to model

As a parent, it is up to you to be the model for healthy boundary setting. It can be hard to practice what you preach, but it is essential for your child to see you both setting boundaries and respecting others' boundaries, too. If your child sees you doing something to someone that would make you angry if they did it to you, then you will lose their trust. The pressure to model these positive traits can be strong.

Finally, while setting boundaries is crucial, it is even more crucial to respect the boundaries that others have set for themselves. This goes for parents, children, romantic partners, bosses, coworkers, and anyone who interacts with or has power over anyone else. Respect is a two-way street, and appreciating the boundaries others have set for themselves is as important as setting boundaries for oneself.

A Few More Tips

Boundaries can be a complex animal, but there are a few miscellaneous tips I'd like to share with you as well that will really come in handy. These tangential thoughts will make going through the steps above even smoother and more effective.

- Make sure the parents are on the same team. Keep parental fights separate and present a united front to your children.
- Ask for and allow your child to share their thoughts on different aspects of their daily lives. You make the final decision, but if they have a request regarding activities or dinner, for example, consider it.
- Avoid very harsh limits or rules that don't have a reason behind them. Kids can see straight through this and it will damage your credibility with them for later.
- Keep adult issues and gossip out of your relationship with your kids.

Practical Positive Parenting

- Be assertive when necessary in a moment that calls for discipline.
- Share time and activities with your child but don't forget that you are the authority.

CALL TO ACTION!

You've probably been tossing around a few ideas in your head for healthy boundaries that you want to set in your family, or perhaps thinking of the boundaries that already exist that just need to be named.

What healthy boundaries do you have in your family? Make a list of the ones you can think of. When you can, ask this question of your child and to your partner, if you have one. Do the answers match up?

If there are boundaries on this list that did not correspond with the answers of your children and partner, or boundaries on the list that get crossed a bit too regularly, set aside time to review them calmly and kindly with your children and partner.

~ 6 ~

STEP #3: PROVIDE WARMTH & STRUCTURE

Now you know your motivation, you know where you want to go, and you have a road map in the form of healthy boundaries. This is where the proactive part of positive parenting begins. The third step to enacting positive parenting is my personal favorite: providing warmth and structure.

It may seem strange to lump together the concept of warmth with structure. The reason I have done so is that both warmth and structure are powerful tools when setting the scene for positive parenting. They both fortify the relationship you have with your child, but in a different way. Warmth, the snuggly feeling that equals love and that children yearn for, is an important base. Structure, in the form of predictability that children often seem to chafe against, is actually something children crave.

Practical Positive Parenting

There will be parts of this chapter that come naturally to you. Other parts will be something new to try, or a new aspect of your family time to be aware of. Take your time reading through and highlighting what you'd like to remember or work on. Remember, there is no shame in finding pieces that are missing from your parenting puzzle.

Providing Warmth: What Does It Mean?

So what do I mean, exactly, when I say provide warmth?

We will get into concrete examples below, but first, let's define it. In Webster's dictionary, warmth is the quality or state of being warm in feeling. I absolutely love, however, the first example the dictionary gives of the word "warmth" in use: "a child needing human warmth and family life." Yes! Right there, Webster's recognizes that one of the most basic ways to employ this term is within the framework of family life.

Think about when you feel the most motivated. Is it when you feel nervous, fearful, or competitive? Or is it when you feel supported by those around you, encouraged to do your best? It's likely the latter. Children are no different. When they are surrounded by warmth and emotional security, children feel safe. They feel safe when they make mistakes, they feel safe trying something out of their comfort zone. If they are afraid of their caregivers, the motivation to try decreases, and they become less confident, as well as less honest. A warm home atmosphere means trusting, confident children who will respect others' feelings.

So how do we show warmth to our children? How do you create the atmosphere we've talked about? Let's explore a few great ways to create warmth in our relationships with our children.

Show love

At its most basic, you provide warmth to your child when you show them they are loved. A hug, saying 'I love you,' taking them to a movie for some quality one-on-one time—all these things are examples of showing love to your child. And if you are doing these things, that's great! But the key part of showing love is making sure that love is received. Have you ever questioned whether your child is receiving all these shows of love on your part?

I absolutely love the concept developed by Gary Chapman and Ross Campbell of the love languages. They've divided shows of love up into five different categories. It is an extremely useful exercise for identifying how you show love, how you receive it, and how your child can receive it. The five love languages they identify are the following: [viii]

- PHYSICAL TOUCH: Every child needs physical touch, of course. However, for a child with this as their love language, a hug or a pat on the back communicates love more deeply than saying I love you or going to the movies. This doesn't mean they won't identify the other types of love. It just means that with physical touch, they hear it loud and clear. Without kisses, hugs, high fives and more, they will be missing something.

- WORDS OF AFFIRMATION: Some children feel most loved when they hear words that affirm them. From 'I love you' to 'Good job today,' for these children, words are very powerful. Quick words spoken throughout the day act as a constant hum of love for these children, and they feel loved for a lifetime.

- QUALITY TIME: This love language is a gift of your, the parent's, time. A child whose love language is quality time needs your undivided attention. With these children, it's not about what you do—it can be homework, playing, or even just going to the supermarket together. They need to feel like they are the center of your world. This is probably the most difficult love language to give.

Practical Positive Parenting

- GIFTS: Yes, some children's love language is actually receiving gifts! All children love gifts, but these children feel a current of love running through that tiny little present. The important thing to note for this show of love is that the gift must not be payment or reward for something, like cleaning a room. A gift is, by nature, unexpected and unconditional.

- ACTS OF SERVICE: As parents, we are serving our children basically nonstop, often during their entire lives. Therefore, it seems to make sense that acts of service should be a love language for many children. However, these acts of service that make children feel loved are often the optional ones. Yes, they will appreciate having dinner on the table every day. But you coming when they call for your help, without complaining, will mean the world to them.

Which of these love languages do you think corresponds to your child? Take a second to identify that. I promise that once you've done so, you'll be able to show love in a much more strategic manner, wasting no effort on your part and making sure your little one feels the most loved they possibly can.

But, above all, the important part isn't *how* you show them you love them—it's being consistent in the doing, day after day.

Build a sense of family

Creating a sense of family is another great way to create warmth.

This is a hugely important piece for most children. Within their family is where children first experience a community. They feel like they are a part of something bigger, and they learn what it means to be giving and altruistic. Belonging to a family helps a child feel recognized and confident, meaning they are more likely to share opinions and participate in group tasks.

Practical Positive Parenting

This sense of belonging to a family has nothing to do with whether you are a nuclear family. It can be a large family, a small family, a single-parent family or a triple-parent family. What matters is that your child feels like they are a part of something. When you ensure that your child knows their place, they will have a positive sense of well-being, which will then absorb into their daily life at home and at school. Here are some great ways to create that sense of family:

- EAT TOGETHER: I love this form of family bonding since it is built into our day's schedule already. There will always be dinner, so why not enjoy it together? Besides sitting down to eat together, distractions removed, you can make the preparations an opportunity for bonding, too. Go shopping together. Cook together. And slightly less exciting but no less effective, clean up together.

- TAKE TIME TO LISTEN: Incorporating moments of being together and just listening can be a great way of connecting and feeling like a family. Don't think that every moment you have to be doing or saying something productive.

- FAMILY MEETINGS: At first, if you are not accustomed to holding family meetings, this one may feel a bit strange, or even forced. Give them a different name, if desired: whether you call it family catch-ups or family time, it is the perfect moment to share how your week has gone, things that you appreciate about each other, and things you are thankful for.

- CHORES: Yes, you read that right. Framing chores as a way to participate in the family helps to create a sense of belonging. Steer clear of assigning them as punishment. Instead, choose an age-appropriate chore for each of your children and frame it as their very own.

Kindness

So much of our behavior within our family is contagious. Have you ever walked in to the house after a hard day of work and felt your spirits lifted by your children playing happily? Or perhaps the reverse is true—it's just as likely you've arrived home ready to play and you find the house suffocated by a hectic, negative atmosphere. Just as moods are contagious, kindness tends to spread among members of the family. That means just a bit of kindness goes a long way.

Kindness is always a bright spot in our hectic lives. When someone is kind to you, it creates a feeling of happiness inside of you, doesn't it? That is powerful. With our actions, we have the power to make others happy. When we project that kindness onto our children, not only are we setting a good example, we are making their world that much happier and brighter.

Kindness also makes you more attuned to the moods and needs of those around you. This compassion makes the world a better place. But it also means your child is more likely to listen to what you have to say. This kindness that helps to show our children love doesn't even have to be directed solely at our children. They are watching our every move. Our kind example will become their kind behavior. Here are some easy ways to add a little kindness to your day:

- Remind your child of things they can do for others, such as sharing, giving gifts, helping with chores. Point out that it makes them feel good, too.
- Think of something you love about your child. Tell them! Don't hold back— really let them feel your admiration and love for them.
- Listen with no agenda. Listen to your child as if they were your BFF venting over the phone. Hold back on any judgment or problem solving unless your child asks directly.
- Read up on positive forms of dealing with arguments and problems. Keep them in the forefront of your mind to use next time you need them.
- Do something kind for yourself! It will put you in the mood to pay it forward. Plus, you deserve it!

Practical Positive Parenting

- If you have to admonish or discipline your child today, do so with kindness: "You may not take your sister's toy, and if you need to talk about anything or want to play with someone, I'm here."

Encouragement

Encouragement is another basic piece of the kindness pie. But how do you show encouragement beyond saying "good job" every now and then?

It's not easy. To start parenting with encouragement, you must first stop judging. Get the words 'good' and 'bad' out of your head when you observe your child's behavior. Instead of thinking of them as either law-abiding citizens or transgressors, think of them as little people looking to find their way. Doesn't that make you want to take their hand, trust in them, and be a positive presence in their life?

Words like "I believe in you" and "you can do it!" play on the innate desire children have to please and to be cooperative. As little people, learning how to be big people, they make mistakes and need our help navigating right and wrong. It's proven that the best way to guide and to help them is by encouraging them. When you encourage your little one to explore, you motivate them to learn.

Here are some simple formulas for replacing certain phrases with more encouraging ones.

DISCOURAGING PHRASE	ENCOURAGING PHRASE
That's impossible!	How would you make it work?
I told you it wouldn't work.	What can we try differently?
I'll do it, I'm faster.	Can you help me, and we'll do it together?
Why did you even bother?	I believe in you.

Practical Positive Parenting

Some other encouraging phrases include:

- Good job!
- I love that idea.
- You got it!
- Keep it up!
- That was awesome! Nice.

Don't forget that an important form of encouragement for your child is to see how encouragement works, by watching its effect on others. To accomplish this, you can point out when others around you encourage and are encouraged. For example, next time your partner, colleague or whoever says something kind to you, you could say, "I felt so good when XXX told me they appreciated my hard work." This will give your child a reference outside of themselves as to how encouragement works.

> CALL TO ACTION!
> Which of the warmth-providing messages resonated with you? Which one do you think you already do a good job with? Which one stuck out to you as having potential for improvement?
> Take that one and brainstorm (writing it down if you can) ways that you can incorporate that type of action into your everyday routine. Try to think of concrete ways that will add warmth to your family environment.

Remember, the important part is to consistently show warmth to your child. Find, by trial and error, the ways that really work with your child and practice them often, and with abandon! Comfort them when they are hurt or afraid, listen to them, play with them, and support them when they experience challenges. Tell them you believe in them, recognize their efforts, and show them you trust them. Anything positive goes!

Practical Positive Parenting

Providing Structure: What Does It Mean?

Structure is the other half of the equation needed to balance things out.

It's different than warmth, but it has a similar effect when we ensure that it has a place in our child-rearing. Children are at their best when they have context clues, information, and help along the way. Structure, in the form of rules, guidelines, boundaries and a routine, can help them immensely in their growth process.

Structure, modeled first by you, the parent, is a beautiful thing. When a child sees a parent following a rule or a routine, it signals to them that this is important. Children are sponges, and they soak that in immediately and use it to make their own decisions.

If we set rules for our children that we do not follow ourselves, or expect them to figure things out and then punish them when they make mistakes, they will feel confused and anxious. If we try to force them to behave in certain ways, they will resist. If we hurt them when they make mistakes, they will become afraid to try. But if we model what we want our children to do and provide the information they need to make good decisions, they will become more confident, competent and independent. As we act as role models, we must explain our rules, listen to any pushback, and help to smooth the way into new routines and teachings.

Here are some great ways to create structure in your children's lives:

Set rules & boundaries

Setting simple, safety-focused limits gives children a sense of structure. See the earlier chapter on healthy boundaries for more detailed information.

Within them, offer freedom

Freedom can be a type of structure. When boundaries are properly in place, giving your children the freedom to express themselves within those boundaries forms a highly functional family structure. Children express their ideas and desires freely within well-set limits, and this makes them feel good, like individuals.

Practical Positive Parenting

Freedom doesn't mean they take over the house and run amok. Freedom comes with responsibilities, and, like adulthood, means being on top of the basics in order to experience that freedom.

The parent-child gap

Part of offering structure is offering a well-defined family hierarchy. You can be close to your child without being their best friend. And you can be a parent that is not constantly dictating and teaching. A closeness, brought about by listening and empathizing, is the ideal relationship between parent and child. Keeping in mind that you are your child's model, while at the same time accepting their authenticity and listening to their deepest thoughts, creates the perfect parent-child dynamic, which is an important part of the structure of the family.

Routine, routine, routine

Children thrive within the boundaries of structure, and in the day-to-day, structure translates as routine. When a healthy routine is in place, daily struggles with pajamas, mealtime, and caregivers smooth out sooner rather than later. Routines make children feel safe. They create these miniature worlds that allow children to transition easily when it's time for a developmental or environmental change.

Not only do they make parents' lives easier, routines help to teach your children important skills. Routines help establish habits, like tooth brushing, and enforce familial contributions in the form of chores. They also help older children to understand time management. The comings and goings of the day have a great effect on children, especially on younger ones, and an established routine is one of the best ways to provide structure to your children.

Another benefit of routines? As a parent, a routine gives you an easy way to structure in some quality time with your child. When stress reigns midweek, it's easy to disconnect and slump into a lump on the sofa. But if you already have built moments of connection into your day, they are there to both save you and comfort you.

CALL TO ACTION!

Building a routine is probably the best way to implement a sense of structure with your children. Do you have a routine? Think about your mornings and your evenings with your children. Make a list, with the approximate times of your routines. Break them down and think about how each aspect of your routine contributes to a sense of warmth and structure.

Take some time to contemplate potential improvements to your routine and ways to incorporate moments that promote a feeling of warmth in your household. Write them somewhere you can reference them easily, such as the Notes app on your phone, and try putting them into action tomorrow.

~ 7 ~

STEP #4: UNDERSTAND HOW CHILDREN THINK & FEEL

You've laid the foundation and set the scene. This is the moment where we begin to prime our characters. By creating an atmosphere in which our children flourish, as we have done in the previous three steps, we achieve a great deal. But now comes the all-important moment of inserting people and real-life situations. Cue the drumroll.

It may sound like this is where things get a bit hectic, but actually, inserting children into your self-aware, warmth-and-structure parenting world doesn't have to knock everything out of place. Taking care to observe Step #4 will make sure to smooth the way forward on your journey into positive parenting.

Practical Positive Parenting

Think about it! How often do we get everything prepared, from our adult point of view, only to remember that we are dealing with a baby, toddler, or child? Our plans will go much better if we do our best to understand our children's natural limits, as well as the motivations behind their actions and their inability to express those motivations fully.

I've seen so many cases where a "misbehaving" child is actually merely mismatched. The expectations of the parent don't match what that child is developmentally capable of. And worse, a parent can get mad under the mistaken belief that their child is purposefully being 'bad,' when often there is just a disconnect in expectations and abilities.

When was the last time you tried to see the world from your child's point of view? I have found this to be the number 1 best way to understand your child's thoughts and feelings. By putting yourself in their place, you understand the reasons behind their behavior and can be a better teacher, too.

Dealing with Difficult Feelings

Challenging moments with our children derive directly from not knowing how to handle difficult feelings. Children are just like adults, in that they can feel angry and frustrated. They have the added stress of not having navigated the emotional and physical world for very many years. This means children do not have the toolkit they need to deal with these hard feelings, and their attempt to do so can often look like acting out.

This moment, the moment of dealing with difficult feelings, has repercussions in their small brains, too. The prefrontal cortex of the brain is in charge of regulating our emotions, an important tool. This part is still developing in young children, a fact which adults must take into account when deciding how to respond to children's "bad" behavior.

Until your child's prefrontal cortex is developed (something that you must help do by modeling) you can expect to see less self-control and more tantrums. The best solution in this interim is to create space between the feelings and the moment. Offer a hug to your child—this will allow them to at least step back from the difficult feelings and the cause of these difficult feelings. Let your child know that it is okay to feel angry/hurt/sad. You can help your child verbalize the root cause of this feeling, while allowing them to process everything and eventually come to terms with their feelings in a way that does not include acting out or throwing a tantrum.

Above all? Try to remain calm yourself. This way, you will give your child an attitude that it is safe and good for them to mirror, which will help them to develop their prefrontal cortex and emotional response. Second of all, a strong emotional response from a parent can actually become a burden on the child.

Stop Talking and Listen

Sometimes we forget the simplest part of making someone feel heard—the listening. As a parent, you absolutely must understand what your child is trying to tell you before you can act or provide a response. What are they really saying when they cry or throw a tantrum? What does that NO really mean? Although it can seem impossible to decipher, taking the time to stop talking and just listen can work wonders when you're trying to understand your child.

Ask the Questions

It may sound obvious, but a great way to start understanding how your child feels and where they are coming from is to ask questions. Getting down to the who, what, and why of their feelings can open up so many doors to understanding them. When you feel that your child has said all they want to say, or if they seem to be waiting on you to chime in or pull something out of them, it's time to get to asking questions.

Practical Positive Parenting

So, what kind of questions can you ask?

- Can you help me understand what just happened?
- What can we do to calm down?
- What's going on?
- Why do you look angry/sad/hurt?

Basically, any open-ended question is a great place to start.

The actual question is less important than the fact that you are asking. Children who are encouraged to listen and respond to open-ended questions actually form a healthier response system to the world around them. The magic of open-ended questions lies in the absence of right and wrong. They help children learn how to think outside the box and develop their ability to express themselves.

One caveat: I do not recommend asking questions in a moment of distress. This can put your child on the offensive, or worse, make them feel attacked and misunderstood before the conversation even starts.

The Steps To Understanding Your Child

Now I'd like to break down the best way to reach understanding of your child. This is important because, let's be honest, in the moment, it can be difficult to remember how to react. But you need to grab ahold of that prefrontal cortex and rein it in, because if you can control your first reaction, you can put into place these four steps to get closer to your child.

Listen

Listening is a key component of conversing. It is the epitome of a first step. Think about it. Would you ever answer someone that asks you a question before that question was asked? The same is true of interaction with your children. Although the situation may not come with a question attached, your child is subtly probing you for answers. So, listen as if there were one—this is how you will get information about what is happening in your child's mental space.

76

Practical Positive Parenting

When listening to your child, it helps to give them your eyes. Look at them. Half of the importance of listening lies in making one party feel listened to. By doing this, you build your relationship with your child and let them know you respect them. And who knows, you might actually learn something! Children are so much more in tune than they get credit for, and they may be able to teach you a thing or two about life!

Another reason listening is an important component of our positive parenting strategy is the mirror effect. As I've mentioned earlier, children look to us and mirror what they see us do. Therefore, listening to your child, and letting them know you're listening, is a great step toward having them listen more to you.

As a parent, you should be always listening. I know you feel you have a hundred different things pulling you in as many directions, but your child may drop hints and ask for your emotional company in strange ways and at inopportune moments. Usually, when you are least prepared.

Reflect

I love this step. I love it because it is simply so easy to put into action, yet so effective. Get ready to have a new favorite tool in the positive parenting arsenal.

The definition of reflecting is paraphrasing what your child says back to them, without interpretation. In action, that means repeating back to them what they said. By simply paraphrasing the words that your child told you, you create a greater sense of closeness and intimacy. Your child feels heard, noticed, seen.

How do you do this, exactly?

The best way to illustrate this concept is by example. If your child says, "I had a horrible day at school, my teacher doesn't like what I do, and she got mad at me." You might say, "You say you think your teacher doesn't approve of your behavior and that makes you feel bad. Is that right?" It's a simple rephrasing of what they have said, bounced back at them with the opportunity to verify tacked on the end. Don't forget to let your child answer that question and adjust, as necessary.

Don't forget to multitask: listen for both facts and emotion. What you need to reflect back to your child is the facts of the situation along with how you think it made them feel. The emotions are as key as what actually happened, so tune in on two frequencies.

And there's a bonus to reflecting your child's emotions back to them. When they hear you describe the problem, it may make it easier for them to come up with a solution on their own. It allows them to put the distance we talked about between them and their strong emotions.

CALL TO ACTION!

Next time your child has a complaint or seems to be upset, focus all your energy on reflecting their words back at them. I want you to focus just on this step so you can feel how different it probably is from your normal reaction. Notice how it feels to say "You feel like your sister is not sharing, which is why you want her toy," rather than "Stop fighting with your sister!"

Try it a few times to really get into the practice of doing it and feeling the difference. I also want you to notice the reaction of your child. Do you notice a visual slackening or relaxing of their body? Do they seem caught off guard?

Once you have practiced this active listening a bit more, then you will be more prepared to run through the full list of steps.

Connect

Once you've passed the steps of listening and reflecting, it's time for the money shot: your chance to connect with your child. Acknowledge their feelings, offer them empathy, and help them feel understood. When they answer your reflection question, it's your chance to connect on a deeper level, really showing your child that their feelings matter to you.

Practical Positive Parenting

Let's see an example.

Child: "I hate my sister! She is always annoying me when I'm trying to play and takes my toys. And you always take her side."

Parent: "It sounds like you are angry that she took your toys and I didn't stop her. Is that right?"

Child: "Yes! I'm so mad!"

Parent: "I'm sorry you're mad. Next time we will tell her to ask you before she touches your things. Do you have anything you could share with her?"

Child: "Maybe…"

Parent: "Is there anything else bothering you?"

Child: "Yes! You always act like she is an angel, and I'm the one who gets in trouble."

In this example, the connection is made with the parent's second statement. The parent empathizes, offers a possible solution, and then hands the solution over to the child to develop. The parent makes no judgment regarding the child's feelings. This is a true, straightforward moment that, when compounded by other similar moments, will teach the child the value of emotional honesty.

When the parent asks "Is there anything else bothering you?" the connection goes deeper. This is, essentially, an invitation for the child to take things further. The parent shows they are ready to listen, and the child will pick up on this and take advantage of it.

Sometimes, even when our children are willing to talk, it can be hard to make that connection. Here are some tips to help you along the way:

- Don't take what they are saying literally. They are likely to exaggerate or use words like "forever" or "never." Your job here is to listen for meaning.
- Watch for nonverbal cues, as well. Sometimes they can say as much or more than words spoken out loud.

Practical Positive Parenting

- Set aside your feelings and your moral beliefs for a second. The goal here is not to judge—it is to gather information in a safe space.
- On that same note, set aside the urge to nag, whether about posture, attitude or anything in between.

Validate

This is the final step in the process of understanding how your child thinks and feels. Validation is the logical next step after listening, reflecting, and connecting. In this context, validation means acknowledging the truth in what your child has said. It can be a single, simple word that confirms to the child that it is okay to have these feelings.

Perhaps this seems like a step that could be skipped or glossed over. However, it is definitely one of the most important pieces of the understanding puzzle. Children are right about how they feel, even if they are working from lack of information or perspective. Their feelings are valid, and it's up to you, the parent, to show them that most of the time.

Kids, especially younger ones, are wont to change their minds. When you validate their feelings, the direction of the conversation pivots away from defense and disagreement and toward a mutual understanding. This may even result in your child retracting a statement or redoing an action, now that they do not feel under attack.

Once you've validated your child's emotions, sit back and see where the conversation takes you, knowing that you've modeled incredible parental behavior.

Practical Positive Parenting

Why Bother?

Understanding how your child thinks and feels isn't just an exercise in futility or mushy parenting. A child who feels understood is a child who will turn to their parent in a moment of real trouble. Following these four steps, which are essentially a breakdown of active listening, will change you and your child's relationship. I promise. You will start to see things that you never saw before. Your empathy will be set into motion as you really, truly see how your little one is affected by something. The positive results will be felt by your child, too.

This type of listening hands some of the power in the conversation to your child. They have the opportunity, when you reflect, to correct your interpretation of their feelings. It will help your child get to know themselves, too. Their often complex and difficult feelings will be easier to decode with your help. This will contribute to a greater sense of self-respect and self-worth. By acknowledging their feelings, you bestow a sense of worthiness onto your child. And when they start to feel more in touch and able to understand their own feelings, their self-respect will skyrocket.

A child who feels understood is also more likely to listen to their parents' advice. That is when all your parenting efforts pay off. Remember, this is a marathon, not a sprint, and the sweat and effort you invest now will pay dividends in the more difficult adolescent years.

From the time your child starts school, their worlds (and their influences) grow at lightning pace. If they have seen you handle problems and stress with grace, they are more likely to do so as well. This is a huge booster for self-esteem, and means your children will see themselves as able to make good choices. In a time of life where independence is so important, they will feel an emotional safety net under them that will really allow them to develop their own decision-making power.

Practical Positive Parenting

When those difficult teenage years come, all this time of making your child feel understood and listened to means that, as your child fights to discover who they are, they will maintain the trust they have in you. They will know that you are there for them, ready to provide honest information and feedback, with clear expectations set. That means that while they are hating music because you love it, or saying things purely to disagree with you, they will know that you are there for them with your same understanding eyes, your same listening ear, and your same supportive embrace.

When these moments come, you will know all your effort was worth it.

~ 8 ~

STEP #5: APPLYING DISCIPLINE IN THE REAL WORLD

"When little people are overwhelmed by big emotions, it's our job to share our calm, not join their chaos."

—— *L.R. Knost*

Welcome to the chapter you have all been waiting for! As with so many things in life, you can't skip over the warmup if you want to reach the finish line. That's why we are talking about discipline in chapter #8 and not #1: the foundation must be laid for it to be effective. That's the same reason why discipline so often fails when parenting—parents neglect to create an environment where discipline will be received by the child, instead relying on imposing their will by force. That only works for so long.

Practical Positive Parenting

You have spent the first part of the book learning what positive parenting is, identifying your goals as a parent, figuring out how you can provide warmth and structure to your children in order to create an environment where they can feel understood. Now it is time to pull this all together in the form of positive discipline.

It's safe to say that discipline is probably most parents' least favorite duty. How many times have you reached the end of the day, only to collapse in exhaustion from having to yell, force, bargain and cajole your children to cooperate? How many times have you felt guilty after an especially tough face-off with your child? How many times have you sworn never to go through a power struggle with a toddler again?

The good news is you don't have to. There is another way: positive discipline.

What is the True Purpose of Discipline?

Before we get into the ins and outs of positive discipline, it is useful to take a step back and look at discipline in general. What is discipline?

According to the Merriam-Webster dictionary, discipline is "orderly or prescribed conduct or pattern of behavior; training that corrects, molds, or perfects the mental faculties or moral character; punishment." Notice that, while punishment is included in the word's definition, it is by no means the sole nor the most important definition of discipline. Rather, discipline has a multifaceted meaning that, to be honest, looks a lot like parenting in general.

The word "discipline" comes from the Latin word disciplina meaning "instruction and training." The root word is actually *discere*—"to learn." Think of the word disciple, which comes from the same root. It's much more about guiding than punishment.

Practical Positive Parenting

It is quite helpful if we disassociate the negative connotations that the word 'discipline' can have. **Discipline is not a bad word.** As long as you have your child with you, as long as they are part of your tutelage, you will be teaching and training them. That is what discipline is about. In modern parenting, it has gotten too attached to the idea of reactionary, negative behavior. In reality, it should be a proactive, positive idea most of the time.

Why Do Kids Misbehave?

It turns out, combining this revised version of discipline with a more complete knowledge of why kids misbehave is a powerful foundation for positive parenting and positive discipline. If you think of yourself as the trainer, rather than the meter of punishments, and you are acutely aware of what is happening with your trainee, things will go much more smoothly.

Let's take a look at the common root causes of misbehavior in children:

- **They don't know better.** This can be possible in younger children. Sometimes they are confronted with a situation that they have never seen before, and they don't know how to react. This innocent misbehavior requires you to tread lightly.
- **Parents expect too much for the child's level of development.** When a young child feels the weight of your expectations, but has not yet hit a developmental milestone that enables them to fulfill your expectations, that can result in them feeling frustrated and impotent—and acting out.
- **They are tired, hungry or have some other physical ailment.** Even adults are subject to this one. Think about how short your fuse is if you haven't had lunch and it's nearly dinnertime. It's nearly impossible for a child to maintain their calm and composure when they are starving or late for a nap, so try to avoid these situations.
- **They want attention.** Giving your child attention when they behave well is super important. If they sense, however, that they are not getting that attention, they can quickly turn to acting up. Whether negative or positive, children have an unbounded need for their parents' attention.

Practical Positive Parenting

- **They're testing boundaries in order to learn**. Kids are programmed to do this. They are little scientists, finding boundaries and then deliberately probing them one by one to test them carefully. They need this firsthand experience to believe in the rules. For children, it's not enough just to rely on what their parents say, at least, not all the time.

- **They are showing their individuality**. Especially in the toddler years, children will act up for no apparent reason. The reason is that they are exerting their individuality. They are showing off that they have autonomous capacity to do whatever they want.

- **They want to know who's in charge**. And, surprise! They want it to be you. Even the most headstrong child wants to feel that surety and strength provided by a caregiver they can depend on. They find comfort when they test you and your boundaries yet you remain calm and in charge.

Positive Parenting Does Include Discipline

Positive parenting often gets a bad rap by those who are unfamiliar with its tenets. A favorite commentary is that positive parenting results in spoiled children who don't face any consequences and do whatever they want. That is sorely misguided.

Positive parenting does include discipline. The major difference in positive parenting and other styles of parenting is its emphasis on the proactive. Positive parenting, as we have seen earlier in the book, puts emphasis on doing all we can to understand our children, an action that we can take at any time, any day. However, when it comes time to correct misbehaviors, positive parents do have disciplinary tools at their disposal.

Positive discipline means providing the warmth and structure we have spoken about in other parts of the book. It means, instead of reverting to pure punishment, the parent approaches the situation with an eye for problem solving and the goal to teach the child what they need to know in the long term, while addressing the momentary problem as well.

Practical Positive Parenting

What Does Positive Discipline Look Like?

No one tries to parent negatively on purpose, right? By parenting negatively, I am referring to common disciplinary methods like yelling, spanking, or even not speaking to your child. They are often methods that just come right out and rear their ugly head before we even give them permission.

Although the name might suggest it, positive discipline is not quite the exact opposite of this strategy. It's not the absence of spanking or yelling that sets positive discipline apart. It is neither permissive parenting nor punishment-free parenting.

So, what exactly is positive discipline?

Positive discipline is a discipline method focused on the positive aspects of children's behavior. The main idea of the method consists of the thought that there is no such thing as a good or bad child, just good or bad behavior. Those who practice positive discipline believe that with enough positive reinforcement, good behaviors can become the default and bad behaviors can be phased out.

Positive discipline is made up of parents clearly communicating appropriate and inappropriate behavior to their children, and at the same time, clearly outlining the rewards and consequences related to these behaviors. In positive discipline, the parent guides the child's behavior while understanding their development and the learning curve they are experiencing. It is a research-based theory, as we have seen previously in the book.

Positive discipline, therefore, offers a long-term solution to children's behavior by developing a self-discipline and respect for others that will serve them their entire lives.

Effects of Positive Discipline

Dr. Jane Nelsen, one of the pioneers of positive discipline and positive parenting, sets out five traits and effects of positive discipline:

- It is kind and firm at the same time.
- It helps children feel a sense of belonging and significance.

Practical Positive Parenting

- It is effective long term.

- It teaches valuable social and life skills for good character.

- It invites children to discover how capable they are and to use their personal power in constructive ways.[ix]

Not only that; she also decries traditional, punitive punishment. Nelsen puts forward several negative consequences of punishment on children:

- Resentment toward parents

- Rebellion against parent's rules and orders, often by increasingly risky behaviors

- Revenge

- Retreat, the child pulling into him or herself and losing self-esteem

As you can see, there is a lot riding on how you respond to your child and how you choose to instruct and train them. This style of discipline is the guiding concept for those who practice positive parenting. Those of us who do practice it are sold on the benefits, but they are also backed up by scientific studies.

These studies have shown myriad benefits when positive discipline is introduced, both at home and in learning environments. They show that a positive discipline style helps children increase their sense of belonging and self-acceptance. It also raises self-confidence and self-esteem.[x] Children just do better when they are reigned over with a firm, kind hand.

How To Implement Positive Discipline

Positive discipline is a concept, not a strategy. It is important to remember that positive parenting is a holistic approach. For positive discipline to work, the other pieces that form the foundation of positive parenting must be in place. For positive discipline strategies to be effective, the child must feel understood, feel respected, and feel upheld by the structure you provide in their life. If necessary, refer back to Chapter 2 for a refresher on what positive parenting consists of.

Practical Positive Parenting

The theory behind positive discipline has been studied and expounded by many people, and from that have been born several books that outline specific techniques for implementing the theory of positive discipline. These books promote strategies about specific, repeatable techniques that use the principles of positive discipline as their foundation.

One great example is *1-2-3 Magic* by Dr. Thomas Phelan, a book that hundreds, maybe thousands of parents swear by. Dr. Phelan has taken the tenets of positive parenting and positive discipline and created a prescriptive reaction that has proved highly effective for many, many children, which I will describe below.

To implement positive discipline, I find it comes in handy to first explore the general steps to its implementation. That way, you know the 'why' behind the various strategies expounded by other books. After reading these steps for implementation, you can pick and choose from various methods of application.

So let's start by going through the steps!

- **Remind yourself of your long-term goals.** Taking a second to gut check what is important to you, and what you want to get across to your child, can serve to reorient the conversation and interaction that you are about to begin. It also helps to avoid going off track and letting smaller, unimportant things distract you from the bigger picture.
- **Consider your child's need to feel respected, understood and loved.** I always think that in a difficult parenting situation, it helps to remember that you are the adult. It helps to call to mind just how vulnerable your child is, and how much they crave your approval and love. When you feel the truth of the situation and the fragility of the life that you have in your charge, it will help to calm and diffuse any anger.
- **Ask yourself questions.** Pose a few key questions to yourself to make progress toward a solution. What would solve this problem from your perspective? What does your child need to solve this situation? What can you do in this situation that will help you toward your long-term goals?

Practical Positive Parenting

- **Consider the child.** How might your child feel as a __-year-old (fill in their age)? Think about their capabilities to understand and act at this stage in their development. By trying to see things from their point of view, you can gather valuable insights about what you should really be expecting from them.

- **Respond with just three things in mind.** Formulate your response with the following things in mind: 1) to inform your child, helping them understand the situation 2) to show respect for your child, and 3) to further your parenting goals.

Now, it's worth commenting that none of this is easy. Some of it may come naturally, and other parts won't. To help you accomplish the transition, it can be useful to practice your responses beforehand for common situations that you find yourself in. Visualize these situations and how you can respond with this toolkit in hand. And remember—this is a learning process. You will make mistakes, but even more importantly, you will learn from them!

Let's look at what these steps can look like when applied to concrete strategies.

A Selection of Positive Discipline Strategies

Here, I will outline a few of the positive discipline strategies I have found to be quite effective. All of them rely on the tenets of positive discipline, but each has their own style and their own technique. Take a look, and see if any of them sound like they may fit your child's personality.

Counting

Above, I mentioned *1-2-3-Magic*, a very popular technique for implementing positive discipline. Dr. Phelan's method consists of counting each time your child makes a transgression. All you, the parent, have to say is "That's 1." And then if the child continues with the bad behavior, "That's 2." Finally, if it continues, "That's 3. Take five." The child is then sent to a time-in/time-out situation, and the problem is diffused for the moment.

Practical Positive Parenting

How is such a simple technique so effective? Phelan says:

> *"Don't worry about feeling skeptical. Remember, the 1-2-3 program is simple, but it is not always easy. The 'magic' is not in the counting. Anyone can count. The magic—or what may seem like magic after you've done it for a while—is in the No Talking and No Emotion rules. Watching you follow these rules makes children think and take responsibility for their own behavior."*

This technique works because it draws on many of the positive discipline tenets. The parent remains calm throughout the process. The 1-2-3 counting is reserved for moments of true misbehaving, not to get your child to do their homework or other mundane tasks. It is applied with consistency, and in a very healthy way, it puts the power in the child's hands.

Redirection

Another example of a method within the umbrella of positive discipline is redirection. Maybe you haven't heard of it, but you have almost definitely used the technique. At its most basic, redirection is a guiding of your child's behavior from inappropriate to appropriate. It can just be a simple, short statement that tells the child what you want them to do.

The book No Drama Discipline[xi] builds on the idea that a moment which calls for discipline is actually better seen as a teachable moment. In this book, Dr. Daniel Siegel has an acronym for REDIRECT that helps break redirection down into actionable steps.

- Reduce words
- Embrace emotions
- Describe, don't preach
- Involve your child in the discipline
- Reframe a no into a yes with conditions
- Emphasize the positive
- Creatively approach the situation
- Teach mindsight tools

Siegel claims that by being consistent and firm, and looking for teachable moments in daily discipline struggles, redirection is an extremely effective form of positive discipline.

The Time-In

The Time-In is another technique widely used by parents in the camp of positive discipline. Dr. Laura Markham, author and childhood behavior specialist, describes time-in as "what it sounds like—the opposite of time-out." Where time-out isolates the child, time-in is a way for you to interrupt "bad" behavior, and to prevent it from escalating, by reconnecting with your child."[xii]

This strategy is based on the precept that, when children get cranky and act out belligerently, it is often because they are trying to deal with built-up feelings from a long day at school or play. This is their way of reaching out to us and saying, "Will you help me with these emotions that I have no idea how to manage?"

What it looks like is the opposite of sending a child to a corner alone, with pent-up anger and frustration that has a new target (*you*). A time-in is you and your child, in a cozy corner specially designated for this situation, with you offering cuddles and connection, along with a firm, fact-based statement (*We do not put our food on the floor*). This will get the point across, but it will also make your child learn how to sit with their emotions, as well as view you on their same team.

And more…

There are definitely other strategies out there when it comes to implementing positive discipline. Fortunately, they are there for you to pick and choose, because you know your child best. I recommend trying strategies at least two weeks before you give up on them.

Continue reading for some general tips on implementing whichever techniques you choose in your positive discipline journey.

Practical Positive Parenting

Tips on Implementing Positive Discipline

Regardless of whether you decide that counting to three or implementing a time-in results in the best response from your child, there are some general tips to getting positive discipline right. The tips I will be sharing below are a treasure trove of hints and how-to's, so read through them carefully and highlight and bookmark away!

Remember, as you read, that children are a world unto themselves. Every child is so very different. I always say that unless someone is in your house with you, day in and day out, they can never know what is best for your child's discipline, health, sleep schedule or anything else. You, the parent, must build the bridge between well-meaning advice and your own child's needs.

Avoid the temptation to look for a one-size-fits-every-situation technique. Just as every child is different, every situation is rife with nuances and may need a slightly different approach to be solved. Positive parenting is, after all, all about tuning in and listening to your child before reacting.

Tips on implementing positive discipline

- Calm down first
- Be aware of nonverbal cues
- Save your words
- Know you can always reconnect later
- Be united with other caregivers
- Be flexible
- Forget about finding a 'magic wand'

Let's delve a little deeper into each of these tips. It is helpful to explain why they are important in order to really understand how they can result in change and reinforce your parenting style.

Calm down first

This one is *so* important. As we have seen throughout the book, a calm parent is an essential piece of positive discipline. On one hand, being calm is important to be able to receive information. You can't be putting out anger at the same time as you are taking in your child's feelings—it's quite literally impossible. On the other hand, being calm in the face of a difficult situation is an incredible way to model the kind of behavior that you would like to see in your children.

So how exactly can you stay calm in moments where you absolutely just want to blow your top?

Start by pausing. Imagine yourself literally pressing a pause button located on your forehead. Everything stops and you become quiet, absorbing everything around you. Breathe deeply until you feel your own emotions start to regulate. Think of it as a parental time-out, if you will.

When you feel a bit of control of your own emotions return, try to remember that your child is too young to be able to manage their feelings effectively.

Remember you have the power in this situation. Act like it.

Be aware of nonverbal cues

Our children know us so well, sometimes speaking is almost superfluous. They are experts in assessing the meaning behind the things we say, synthesizing it with our past actions and our current body language. The importance of nonverbal cues, which include body language but also include paralanguage such as tone of voice, cannot be overstated. Our children may be small, and they may not have studied much, but they are scarily in tune with what our nonverbal cues are saying.

What we do, therefore, is much more important than what we say, especially when it comes to our children. This makes sense; children are born without knowing any words, and their experience of emotion is, for many months, nonverbal. That is how they learn to love. You want to be sure that your nonverbal cues are— 1) communicating what you want them to, and, 2) are in line with your verbal communication as well.

Nonverbal cues are your friends. They are incredibly powerful, so use them to your advantage!

How to evaluate your own nonverbal cues can be a bit tricky, as you are coming at the situation quite literally from the inside. To help discern your nonverbal contribution to the situation, ask yourself:

- Did your child pay attention and do as you asked?
- Apart from what you said, what other nonverbal cues did you send out?
- Which nonverbal cues are your favorites or the ones you usually employ? How many times a day do you use them?

Practical Positive Parenting

Save your words

There is most definitely a time and a place to explain within the framework of positive parenting. However, during a situation that requires disciplinary action on the part of the parent is not that time. Excessive explanations in this type of moment distracts children—from the discipline, yes—but even more importantly, it distracts children from their own feelings. The natural feeling of guilt, or that uh-oh feeling that is so strong in most children, is a great natural disciplinary tool. Taking a disciplinary situation too cerebral can mute its effectiveness.

Also, studies have proven that children need that break from excessive explaining to process what is happening. They show that too many words and complicated phrases from the parent has a distracting, confusing effect, making them less likely to eventually abide by your disciplinary orders.

Another positive aspect of saving your words? It gives you that much more bandwidth to listen with. Listening more than you talk is a powerful tool in disciplinary moments. A child who feels like they are being listened to is more likely to listen and cooperate themselves.

Know you can always reconnect later

Oftentimes, the difficulties we feel disciplining our children come from our own anxieties. Will my child love me the same if I discipline them? Will they think that I don't love them? Will it hurt our relationship? All these questions can rebound around in your head and drive even the most confident parent a bit insane.

But get this: You can always reconnect with your child later. Regardless of whether this moment feels uncomfortable or makes you feel guilty, these types of moments are common and do not mean any sort of long-lasting damage is imminent. The best thing you can do as a parent is wait for things to settle and then carefully choose a moment to reconnect (with a chat, a hug, or whatever else comes naturally) with your child.

Practical Positive Parenting

Doing this will reinforce for your child that moments of discipline do not reflect on your parent-child relationship. It will also make your child feel important in your eyes, by virtue of you taking the time out of your schedule to reconnect.

Be united with other caregivers

This is a complaint I hear every now and then, and, boy, is it a tough one. All of the concepts I've addressed earlier are so much easier to put into place when consistency is there and children are not getting mixed messages. That's why it is important to present a united front with your partner, your child's other parent, or the other main caregivers in your child's life.

In the case that you and your partner mostly agree on child-rearing, congratulations! You are in luck. That means this whole journey is going to be a lot smoother. Not smooth, mind you—but having the same opinion on how to react when your child needs disciplining is a great step toward implementing effective positive discipline.

Perhaps you and your partner do not agree on the what, but you do agree on the how. This is the next-best scenario: when partners don't agree on discipline but know that it's important to keep that disagreement behind the scenes. Do not fret if this is you. A willingness to agree to disagree is huge.

There are a few key rules that can help you form a united front with your partner even when behind-the-scenes unity is nonexistent.

- Rule #1: If one parent disciplines the child, back them up. If you disagree, talk it out later When in front of the child, act like a team.
- Rule #2: If there is something especially important to one of the parents, try to let them "win" that one. It won't always be this easy, but by ceding things that aren't quite as important to you, you can win battles down the road.
- Rule #3: Talk over parenting decisions when you are both calm and collected. There's no point in getting into a huge argument in the heat of the moment— that will benefit neither you nor your child.

Practical Positive Parenting

Perhaps you are in the unenviable position of having a partner with whom you do not see eye to eye. And on top of that, perhaps this partner does not want to cooperate with you. Whatever your situation may be, know that it is possible to discipline your child the way you believe they should be disciplined, even without your partner on board. The bad news is that it will take a will of iron from you to maintain the consistency of your approach in the face of opposition. The good news is you can be sure that your child will eventually find themselves gravitating toward your consistency.

Be flexible

After all that talk about consistency, it might seem like flexibility is counterproductive. Nothing, however, could be further from the truth. Consistency builds the foundation and creates a sense of predictability, which children need and cherish. However, it can also easily turn into rigidness.

That is one thing we want to avoid: flexibility is our friend. Having flexibility allows you as a parent to consider what is best for your child in different situations. When your child does something their way, having flexibility allows you to stop, think about it, and decide if you really need to step in.

Acting out of flexibility also shows your child that you are willing to take exceptional circumstances into account. This makes your child feel more secure, and can even strengthen the trust your child feels in you. It also helps you give yourself permission to adapt to the changes you see in your child.

Apart from the obvious relaxing of rules and consequences according to a worthy situation, there are many ways to incorporate flexibility into your parenting. For example, you can make a special effort to allow your children to do things themselves, biting your tongue when it's not quite perfect as long as no harm is done. You can make a special mental effort to view your child's feelings from a place of authenticity, and not from a place of misbehavior. You can also involve your children in decision making whenever possible.

All of these are great ways to put flexibility into action.

Practical Positive Parenting

Forget about finding a 'magic wand'

Sometimes the roadblocks to implementing discipline are not our children; they are ourselves. As parents, it's easy to find ourselves clinging to beliefs or behaviors that are actually quite counterproductive. One of those beliefs that I see all the time is the belief that there is a single, magical way to control your child and enact discipline. I think we know with our brains that this is not so. However, for those that don't, just think about it: if there were, wouldn't we all be doing it? If there were a definitive solution, its creator would be the parenting god. And…there's not.

Even though we know with our brains that there is no one-size-fits-all solution, sometimes we still long for there to be. Clinging to that belief is an impediment to moving on to something that really works. The best thing you can do is forget about the 'magic wand' and get down to business.

Relationships with your children are complex, and that's okay. One size will never fit all, and the sooner you come to terms with that fact, the better. Sometimes, your best won't be enough to calm your child, so don't beat yourself up about that.

Persistence, love and a desire to learn and grow as a parent is the 'magic wand' everyone is looking for.

The End Goal

The end goal of positive discipline is teaching your child to be a responsible, self-aware being. I believe that the use of positive parenting and positive discipline helps to foster a better relationship between parent and child, which makes child-rearing an overall more enjoyable experience.

With positive discipline, we teach our children that they must be accountable for their actions. However, we also teach them the very important accompaniment to this: that they are immensely capable of doing so. This is the end goal of our parenting.

Practical Positive Parenting

One last word: It may seem sometimes like you just can't do the right thing. Anytime that feeling strikes, please remember that being perfect isn't what parenting is about. Parenting is about doing the best you can, and when that isn't enough, showing your children what dealing with mistakes looks like. We aren't preparing our children for a perfect life with no challenges, after all—we should be preparing them for the moments that will be more difficult or moments when their best effort doesn't work.

SECTION THREE

~

THE 10 COMMANDMENTS TO PARENT BY

"Raise your words, not your voice. It is rain that grows flowers not thunder."

— *Rumi*

Practical Positive Parenting

~ 9 ~

AGES 2-4: THE TEN COMMANDMENTS FOR DISCIPLINING TODDLERS

Disciplining children, as I have mentioned earlier, has many different techniques and formats. That is why it's useful to find a disciplinary concept that you like and then build on that with your own methods. The previous chapter contains tips in implementing discipline in ways that will help, not hurt, your chances of success and your relationship with your child.

The next two chapters are made up of what I call the "ten commandments of positive discipline," broken down by age group. This chapter is especially effective for toddlers from two to four years old, although I encourage you to read both chapters 9 and 10 regardless of the age of your child. The commandments each include useful, real-life examples that will help you apply them in your own life.

Practical Positive Parenting

You and your child's personalities are important factors in how you communicate and interact. If you are quiet and your child is, too, your relationship might have many more moments to connect and cuddle. If you are rigid, you may tend to impose rules more frequently, and if your child does not like structure, that can create quite the problem. The temperament of your child has a big effect on how you react, so keep your personal preferences in mind as you read through these commandments.

If you follow these ten commandments when dealing with your child, however, I can guarantee a better result. You will see improvement in the form of better behavior on the part of your child, as well as an increased closeness in your relationship. The key is in the tenth commandment, however: this will take time, so be patient and consistent.

As an overview, the ten commandments for disciplining toddlers are as follows:

#1 Respond to the Good in Your Child
#2 Show Understanding & Compassion
#3 Reflect Their Feelings Back at Them
#4 Project Calm
#5 Focus on What the Child Can Do
#6 Get on Their Level
#7 Don't Back Down to Avoid Conflict
#8 Give Your Child Choices
#9 Consistency Counts
#10 Results Take Time

Practical Positive Parenting

#1 Respond to the Good in Your Child

Your child craves your attention. Choosing how to dispense it can be the most powerful tool in positive parenting, which is why this is the number-one commandment. Responding to the good in your child means giving them positive attention, showing them they have done something you like. This replaces the knee-jerk reaction many parents have of calling out bad behavior, also known as negative attention.

Responding to the good in your child can look like simply recognizing good behavior and commenting on it, or you can use positive reinforcements like hugs, pats on the back, kisses or a high five. This not only motivates your child to good behavior; it also helps to build self-esteem.

In Real Life...

You are waiting in line at the drugstore with your child. He waits by your side, patient except for the occasional tug at your shirt, which he does inadvertently but you can just barely feel it. You tell him, "Thank you for waiting so patiently with me." When you tell him, you are looking in his eyes and you give him a warm smile. He smiles back, and even the inadvertent tugging stops.

Practical Positive Parenting

#2 Show Understanding & Compassion

This commandment is a double-edged sword. By showing your toddler that you understand her, you will create a stronger, more trusting bond between the two of you. But that's not all. When you show understanding and compassion, you are modeling empathy for your child. Learning empathy is an important part of her journey to being an older child.

So how do you show understanding and compassion to a toddler? Notice when they express emotions. Stop what you are doing and look at them. For toddlers, eyes equal attention. Ask them questions about their feelings—and listen to the answer. Offer to hold them while they're showing that emotion. Not literally, necessarily, but just being by their side as they experience the emotion is often enough. This reaction is far preferable to that of diminishing your child's anger or fear by telling them 'not to worry' about it.

In Real Life...

> Tom is walking down the street with his daughter, Trina. A neighbor is walking toward them with his German shepherd. The dog starts to bark and pull wildly at his leash. Trina jumps and starts wailing, hiding behind her dad's knees. Tom waits for the neighbor to pass with the dog. He turns to Trina. "Are you feeling scared?" he asks her. She nods. "He's a sweet dog, but he is barking so loud! I got scared, too. Let me give you a big hug until you feel less scared." Trina gives her dad a big hug. "I feel better now," she says.

Practical Positive Parenting

#3 Reflect Their Feelings Back at Them

Reflection is an important step in your toddler's growth. When you reflect their feelings back at them, you give the feeling a name, one that may often be a new notion to your tot. This reflecting and talking helps them to put their feelings into words, both validating and encouraging them to share their feelings. The more skills you share with your child when it comes to a healthy expression of emotion, the fewer kicks or tantrums will be necessary to get them across.

Building their vocabulary begins with the words we use to describe and explain intensity.

Four-year-old Al is a blond, tousle-haired mini-tornado. "I've got gusto," he informed me. "My dad says it's okay to do things with gusto—as long as you don't hurt anybody!"

"I'm full of it," a five-year-old shared, "just like my Grandpa Rick."

"My mom plays whisper games with me to help me practice my soft voice because usually I've very dramatic," six-year-old Libby exclaimed.

In Real Life...

You're playing with your toddler after lunch. Your child calls out to you. "What, honey?" you say. "I'm hungry!" she says.
"Hungry?" you ask. "You can't be hungry! We just ate lunch."
"But I AM!" your toddler says.
"You just ate!" you insist.
"I'M HUNGRY!" your toddler says, pounding the ground with her foot. She bursts into tears and begins a general meltdown.
Now, let's rewind that a bit and see how it can change when you reflect their feelings back to them, rather than telling them you know better.
Your child calls out to you. "What, honey?" you say. "I'm hungry!" she says.

Practical Positive Parenting

"So, you're still hungry even though we just had lunch," you say.

"Yes!" your toddler agrees, looking a little less anxious.

"Okay," you say. "If you are hungry, in a little while we can have a snack."

"Okay," she says. You both continue playing together.

Practical Positive Parenting

#4 Project Calm

Children often follow our cues, looking to adults to model the correct behavior. This commandment is another golden one. If we, as adults, project calm despite being angry, we are helping diffuse the current situation and simultaneously modeling emotional intelligence for our children.

So how do you stay calm? A huge key is to realize your child's behavior is something that may or may not have to do with you. It is so often based on external factors, from hunger to biology. Sometimes, taking the burden for our child's behavior off our shoulders does a lot to ease our haunting feelings of guilt or inadequacy. Once that haunting feeling of "she's trying to manipulate me" or "he's testing me" or "I'm not good enough for him" is dismissed, you may find that you are much less likely to explode at your child's perceived misbehavior. This is called depersonalizing, and it prevents you from feeling personally attacked. It makes it so much easier to remain calm and stay engaged with your child's feelings.

The importance of modeling calm behavior in the face of emotional upset cannot be overstated. Your child is learning by watching you! What are you teaching them?

In Real Life...

Sarah is getting her son, Sam, ready for daycare. It's the beginning of the new school year, and Sam loves his daycare. The first week went incredibly smoothly. But then, one morning, she is helping Sam get ready. She leaves the room, asking Sam to pick out a shirt to wear. When she returns, all of his shirts are on the floor and he tells her he can't choose one.

Instead of yelling at Sam, which is her first instinctive reaction, Sarah checks herself. She thinks about how it must feel to go to nursery all day after a summer spent at home with family. She bites her tongue. Sam isn't trying to upset her or make her late. He's just unable to deal with his feelings.

Practical Positive Parenting

"You do have a lot of cool shirts, Sam," she says. She goes over and gives him a big hug. "What about this one?" She holds up the shirt she knows is Sam's favorite. She helps him put it on and gives him another hug. "Now why don't you pick up the shirts and put them back in the drawer." Sam does it and then goes to breakfast and happily to school.

Practical Positive Parenting

#5 Focus on What the Child Can Do

The fifth commandment is to focus on what your child can do, rather than emphasizing the 'no' or 'don't.' Telling your child (often, over and over again) to stop doing this or that is an ineffective form of discipline. It may work for a while, but that will change sooner or later (or your child will end up resenting you). Plus, often children aren't sure what behavior to substitute instead. Above all, it's also pretty tiring, as any parent can attest to.

Focusing on what the child can do is a proactive way to guide your child toward desired behavior. You want to be as specific as possible so your child can easily adopt your suggestions. This commandment, which is a combination of positivity and redirection, lies at the very foundation of positive discipline.

In Real Life...

Your child is running around like a wild man. You watch him turn corners with ever-growing speed. You imagine a collision with the corner of a table.

"Stop running in the house!" you say.

"No!" he shouts, as he continues on his merry way.

Let's rewind and try focusing simply on the facts and what your child can do. Begin your statement with a fact or neutral statement. Here we go:

"It is not safe to run in the house," you say. "Please go to the backyard if you want to run." Notice that at no point did you tell your child what not to do, nor did you come at him personally, which can feel like an attack for little children.

"Okay!" he says, changing course and running right out to the back patio.

Practical Positive Parenting

#6 Get on Their Level

This is one of my favorite commandments, and not only because it works! I love this commandment because it's so physical and easy to execute. The concept is this: when you are communicating with your little one, bend over or squat down so that you are able to be close to them, eye to eye. It's incredible how something so simple can be so effective.

Why does it work? If you put yourself in your child's shoes, it's not hard to see why. Imagine being towered over, versus being on the same physical level as someone. This trick is shown to make children feel safer, more in control and connected.

Top it off with a calm tone and a low volume and this physical tool can get real results. Do not use baby talk—use short, simple sentences or even single words to maximize your child's attention. You will convey to your child that you are there for them, paying attention and listening.

In Real Life...

Don is taking care of his 2-year-old Tina for the day. They go to an ice cream shop after about an hour of playing in the park. Don tells Tina they can get an ice cream cone and that she can pick it out. When the server asks what ice cream they would like, Don orders a chocolate ice cream cone, which he knows is Tina's favorite. The server begins preparing the ice cream. Tina, however, gets upset.
"You said I could pick it out!" Tina cries.
"Isn't chocolate your favorite flavor?" asks Don.
"I want to pick out the ice cream! You said I could!" Tina is shouting now, and has tears forming in her eyes.
"It will be delicious, sweetie," says Don. Tina is sweaty and tired from the park. She begins to wail.
Don bends down to her level. He makes eye contact with Tina and is very still. Tina stops wailing.

Practical Positive Parenting

"I know you are tired from our long day," says Don. "And I know you wanted to pick out the ice cream. Am I right?" Tina sniffles and nods.

"What flavor did you want?" asks Don.

"You mean I can pick it out?" asks Tina.

"Yes," says Don. Tina wipes her face off and looks into the glass display case. Don peers in right next to her. She turns sheepishly to him.

"I want chocolate," she says. Don gives her a hug and hands her the cone from the server's outstretched hand.

Practical Positive Parenting

#7 Don't Back Down to Avoid Conflict

An essential part of positive parenting is being able to discern the difference between flexibility and backing down. There will be times that your child doesn't follow your instruction or acts out as a way to test your limits. That's what little children do—they are like scientists, forming mini experiments that often drive you crazy, just to see if the results will differ. There will be other times, however, that your child may just be hungry, tired, or honestly unable to do what you ask of them. Knowing your limits and communicating them is important, because this is how you will be able to make the call: should I be flexible, or is this a conflict that I must weather to show my child that these limits exist?

If you feel that it is the latter, then this is a time where you should stand your ground. It is time to be kind, yet firm. In these moments, think of your child as part of the family, not the center of the world. What is best for them? Once you make this decision and settle on what you are going to do, it's vital to stick with it. Do not say you are going to do something and then not follow through in order to avoid conflict.

In Real Life...

Jen and her just-turned-two-year-old baby John began to have trouble at diaper changing time. John wanted to wriggle and fight when it was time for a new diaper. Often, he would move so much that Jen simply couldn't get his diaper changed. At first, she asked him, cajoled him, and even begged him to sit still, which seemed to make him wiggle even more furiously.

Practical Positive Parenting

Then, Jen decided she wasn't going to fight John's 'spirit' anymore. She told him, "I need you to help me. If you don't stop moving, then I can't change your diaper and we can't get up and play." Whenever John started wriggling and fighting the diaper change, she would stop and sit patiently, waiting for him to finish. As soon as he was still, she continued with the change. She never showed any emotion or impatience. Soon enough, John got bored with the wiggling gig and began to allow his diaper to be changed without incident. It wasn't long before he was toilet trained, too.

Practical Positive Parenting

#8 Give Your Child Choices

Giving your child the choice between two options is a very effective discipline technique. This staves off two often-overwhelming scenarios for children: 1) feeling cornered into doing something they don't want to do, or something they simply don't want to be told to do; 2) feeling overwhelmed by being offered too many options or an open-ended "what do you want to do?" Too much freedom does not actually make your child feel free—it leaves a child feeling stressed and unsure of themselves.

By offering a couple choices, your child will feel as if they have a say in what is going on. The key to making this commandment work is to be sure the two choices you offer are actually acceptable outcomes for you, as well. That means not giving your child the option to brush their teeth or not, but instead offering a choice of toothpastes, for example. This is a way to create an empowered, cooperative child. Just imagine, every time that you use this technique, adding a block to the base of your child's future self and self-esteem. We create capable adults when we allow our small children to begin to make their own decisions.

In Real Life

Your little one is in a phase where he never stops moving. He wants to run, nonstop, everywhere. You can already tell you're raising an independent spirit, which is exciting for you. However, there are moments in which safety is an issue. You tell him to slow down, to wait for you or to do something else, and he either runs off or says he doesn't want to do that.

You are out and about with your little one. It's been a long day and you can sense he is pretty close to a meltdown. You decide it's best to head for the car and you come to a pedestrian crossing. You reach for his hand and he pulls away.

Practical Positive Parenting

"Honey," you say, calmly, "would you like to hold my right hand or my left hand when we cross the street?" Your toddler considers carefully and shouts "RIGHT!" Crisis averted, by not giving him time to consider the non-option of not holding your hand at all. Good job!

Practical Positive Parenting

#9 Consistency Counts

I've said it before, but I really do think of children as little scientists. It is their job to push you and see if they can get you to change your mind. And who can fault someone for just doing their job? I find reminding myself of this fact to be super helpful in keeping calm and applying my rules consistently. I've saved this commandment for nearly the end because it technically applies to all the previous commandments. Whatever you do, try to be as consistent as you can when you do it.

That's it! There's nothing magic about this one. It's just putting in the time, taking one step forward, and then another, and then another. If you do find yourself falling off the wagon or having a hard day, don't worry. Inconsistency is normal when something has yet to become a habit. You aren't perfect, and your kids don't need you to be. Life is complicated, so forgive yourself and start again!

In Real Life...

> You know a consistent bedtime would help with getting your child to sleep, but you just can't seem to make it work. You have work deadlines, older kids' practices, or other important things to take care of in the evenings, and sometimes you just can't get your kid to bed on time. That means announcing bedtime nearly always causes a meltdown.
>
> In this scenario, you can still achieve consistency. Embrace the consistency of a range of acceptable outcomes. Instead of insisting that bedtime is at 7 p.m. sharp, set a range of time that is acceptable for bedtime, for example, 7 p.m. to 8 p.m. This helps when external circumstances cause unexpected changes in your family's schedule. Couple that with a consistent bedtime routine, and I'm sure that bedtime will become a whole lot easier for your family.

Practical Positive Parenting

#10 Results Take Time

This is, technically, not a commandment for action—more like a commandment for inaction. When applying all these commandments above with your child, don't expect an overnight solution. There will be some setbacks along the way, and you may even feel that things at some points get worse. The important thing to remember here is to stay the path and be consistent.

Especially if your child is used to receiving a different type of discipline from you, the change will take some time to go into effect. Your child will naturally push back a bit at first, and you will be new at this and not always equipped to respond in the best way. Grant yourself a little bit of grace and continue doing the best you can!

Practical Positive Parenting

~ 10 ~

AGES 5-7: THE TEN COMMANDMENTS FOR DISCIPLINING OLDER CHILDREN

"Respect your kids. Too many adults demand respect from kids without showing any respect in return. It doesn't work."

—— *Lyle Perry*

Children develop so quickly, passing through truly different phases in their journey from toddler to "big kid." That's why there are two "ten commandments" chapters—what works for a 2, 3, and 4-year-old, just doesn't have the same effect on a 5,6, and 7-year-old.

Disciplining older children is very rewarding. It has its challenges, but the introduction of the capacity to reason into your child's development timeline is an incredibly helpful development. From 5 years old, children are much more able to exert self-control, show independence, and follow direction. They are, however, also more apt to test boundaries and demand to do it themselves.

Practical Positive Parenting

Hopefully, you've been building a foundation with your child over the past few years. This will make the discipline during this period that much smoother. That said, it's never too late to start positive parenting, so jump right in to this set of ten commandments. If you skipped the previous chapter because you have an older child, I encourage you to read both chapters 9 and 10 regardless of the age of your child. You may just glean an important piece of advice that still works like magic with your older child. The commandments each include useful, real-life examples that will help you apply them in your own life. And I'll reiterate: your child's personality has a big effect on what discipline they will respond to, so keep your personal preferences in mind as you read through these commandments.

As an overview, the ten commandments for disciplining older children are as follows:

#1 Use Your Attention

#2 Incorporate Routines That Promote Good Behavior

#3 Create Clear Limits

#4 Save Your No's

#5 Ask Questions

#6 Offer Do-Overs

#7 Explain Why

#8 Try A Behavior Management System

#9 Set Time To Connect

#10 Encourage Independent Problem Solving

Practical Positive Parenting

#1 Use Your Attention

I'm kicking off the ten commandments for older children with the most strategic point. You, as a parent, have one currency: attention. Think of your attention like the money in your bank account. With your money, don't you decide carefully and pointedly how to spend it? Do you spend your money on things you don't enjoy, like, or need? If you're anything like most humans, you choose not to spend your money on things you don't think are worth it.

Your attention, when it comes to your child, should be spent the exact same way. Your child is hungry for that attention, so if you can make it clear to them that good behavior equals attention, and bad behavior gets none, they will likely be quick to give up on the bad behavior. Attention-seeking behavior is right on target for this age group, and it's a need that can feel as physical as hunger. Studies have shown it lights up the same areas of the brain!

In Real Life...

Mark and his sons William and Bo are at the library. They are choosing books to take home for the weekend. Mark is looking over a book that Bo has found and telling him how cool it looks. William is looking at easier books on the other side of the aisle.

"Dad!" says William. "Come see the book I found!"

"One second," says Mark.

William starts pushing the books through so that they fall to the floor, one by one. He watches Mark to see his reaction. Lately, Mark and his wife have been careful with how they apply their attention to William, as he tends to act out when he feels he doesn't immediately get the attention he wants. They have been working with him to encourage him to use a polite phrase ("Excuse me, Dad!") instead of doing something he's not supposed to. William understands but is still learning and testing boundaries.

Practical Positive Parenting

Mark continues commenting on the book Bo has in his hands. Bo is watching Mark, too. William pushes two more books to the floor. He stops, watching Mark read to Bo. He walks around to the two and says, loudly, "Excuse me, DAD!"

Mark turns to William and says, warmly, "Hey Will, what do you need?"

"I want to show you a book TOO!" says William, still a little loud.

"Sure! Let's pick up these books first, though," says Mark. William helps him shelve the books and the two go see the book William has picked out.

#2 Incorporate Routines That Promote Good Behavior

Creating routines is one of the best ways to get cooperation from your child. Once you settle on a routine with your child, the routine takes the reins and the parent is no longer the boss of the situation—i.e., there is no one to argue with. Children like to know what to expect. It gives them a sense of security in a world that, from their point of view, is always changing. While routine may have seemed to be a synonym for boring to your pre-child self, you will find that routines are actually powerful things.

Consider creating a routine for the most problematic of daily situations. If morning is a struggle, create a morning routine and try to make it a bit fun by using drawings, stickers or cards. If bedtime isn't working, try a series of steps to complete before every bedtime to wind your child down. An important part of incorporating routines is allowing your child to take charge of its pieces. That way your child will feel the weight of the routine, and any chance for a power struggle between you and the child will be diminished.

In Real Life...

Emily's child has been resisting the mornings since school started this year. What was already going to be a tough transition, to "big kid school" has turned into a daily wrestling match where she has to try to remember everything on her morning to-do list as well as that of her daughter. She buys some picture cards that feature everything on their morning to-do list: Brushing teeth, Combing hair, Washing face, Getting dressed, Eating Breakfast, Putting shoes on, Grab backpack/lunchbox. She sets them up with magnets and talks them over with her daughter, Delia. She walks Delia through it the first day. Delia is fascinated!

The second day, she goes to help Delia to remember the order of things. Delia tells her, "I don't need you, I can do it myself." She completes her routine without a word and is ready to go to school on time.

Practical Positive Parenting

#3 Create Clear Limits

We've already talked a lot about the importance of setting boundaries in this book (see Chapter 5). Creating clear limits is a similar concept. Limits are effective for many of the same reasons that routines are: they let your child know what to expect. Too much freedom can feel overwhelming for children, and can even cause them to act out for attention. Too much structure and no flexibility can cause them to rebel. Your limits should ideally land somewhere in the middle, always with the ultimate goal of keeping your child safe.

You want to be certain and firm when you communicate these limits, so be sure that when you create the limits, they are good ones. A good limit is: 1) clear; 2) reasonable; 3) attainable. It's also very helpful to write down the most important ones in a simple list—this helps everyone to remember them, including adults. And remember to be aware, because as your child grows, some limits will need to grow along with them!

In Real Life...

Screen time is becoming a struggle in your household. The older your child gets, the more they want your phone or the family tablet. You find your child sitting with it almost any time you leave them alone. Time to set some limits. First, you communicate your clear limit, telling your child that they may use electronics for thirty minutes and then they must be turned off. Then, you communicate what will be the consequence for breaking the limit, telling them that if they don't turn off the electronics when the time is up, you will put them away for the rest of the day and tomorrow. You tell them the when, as well, saying that if they refuse to end screen time, you will know they are choosing to lose their privileges for the next two days. By framing it as a choice, you put the power in your child's hands to follow your limits, and the most likely outcome is that, after a few tests, they will eventually do so.

Practical Positive Parenting

#4 Save Your No's

We all know that the more you have to exert power over your child, whether it be by traditional punishment, a battle of the wills, or saying no, the less impact these means have on your child. That is why one of the commandments, especially for children in the 5-7 age group, is to save your "no's" whenever possible. Otherwise you risk desensitizing your child to its importance.

But how do you save your no's" exactly? For one, be sure to cull all those unnecessary no's. If it really won't do any harm if your child does X, then let them. At the risk of being mildly irritated, it's better to save those powerful no's.

It helps to look at the times you have to say no. Usually, these are circumstances of problem solving. If you work on solving problems together with your child, you put in place a process that is much more effective than overusing no. This process is quite different than the way you may have learned from your parents: no negotiation, no say, just their way or the highway. The good thing is, this can help smooth our relationship with our kids over the long term.

All it takes is understanding your child's feelings, gently explaining why they are incompatible with the bigger picture, and following through.

In Real Life...

Adam is at home with his two children, Daniel, five years old, and Mary, three years old. Mary grabs one of Daniel's toy cars and starts playing with it. "Hey!" shouts Daniel, right before he slaps Mary a bit hard on the hand. Adam, who is sitting with them, sees this happen and remembers that he is trying to save his no's. He separates Mary a bit from Adam after making sure she is fine.
Adam says "We use our words, not our hands."
Daniel looks at Adam, his chin shaking a bit.
"If you are angry, use your words, not your hands. Do you understand?"

Practical Positive Parenting

"Yes," said Daniel. Adam gives him a hug. Instead of saying "no hitting," he helps Daniel know what to do with his anger and how to better channel it.

Practical Positive Parenting

#5 Ask Questions

Ask questions. As a positive and responsive parent your job needs to be to put yourself in your child's shoes, to feel what they are feeling. To do so, the best, quickest way is to ask questions. By showing interest in your child's feelings and asking for more details, you're helping them feel held and seen.

What kind of questions? Well, that is where there is one caveat: there are two questions I try to avoid using whenever possible in the case of dueling siblings or friends: "who started it?" and "what happened?" When there are two children involved, the likelihood of you getting to the bottom of anything by asking either one of them a question is very, very slim. Avoid those two questions, which almost always lead to confusion.

Instead, use your questions to find out what is happening from your child's point of view. It helps to start by reflecting their feelings back at them and then asking a non-judgmental question. For example, "You aren't usually like this, what's wrong?" will probably elicit some kind of positive exchange between the two of you.

In Real Life...

You are riding home from school with your seven-year-old. Out of nowhere, she says "My friends are so boring." While your instinct may be to tell her not to say mean things about others, or otherwise try to cheer her up immediately, you decide to practice the asking questions commandment.

"You don't usually say that," you say. "What's up?"

"I wanted to play a new game at recess and they wouldn't," she says.

You nod, and she continues telling you about her day at school. Instead of making her feel isolated by reproaching her, or making her feelings feel unjustified by cheering her up, you are having a conversation about something you otherwise would have had no idea happened. That's a win!

Practical Positive Parenting

#6 Offer Do-Overs

Offering do-overs may sound to some like a softy option. What's done is done, and children should have to take ownership of their actions. Right? Well...ownership yes, but if you just stop at the lesson and the consequences, you miss an opportunity for learning and for practice. Instead of beginning a lecture or leaving your child with too little information after disciplining, give them the chance to redo their response in the form of a do-over.

When you offer a do-over, you create a new opportunity to connect with your child. The struggle that is at the heart of the problem is suddenly shifted out of the spotlight. Without allowing the situation to escalate, you provide a learning "out" for your child. You give your child the gift of actually practicing the desired response, of feeling how it feels to say it, of watching the reaction of the affected person. It's motor memory at its best, and the best way to teach and train for desired behavior.

In Real Life...

Kathy is a kindergarten schoolteacher, and faces a lot of challenging childhood scenarios. One of her favorite strategies is the do-over. During show and tell one day, one of the boys in her class gets very excited about the army man that another is showing off. He grabs it from his neighbor. Kathy jumps in and says "Oh, Ian, you are very excited, I can tell! Let's try that again with more respect for your neighbor." Kathy hands the army man back to the other boy. "Can I see the army man, too, please?" asks Ian. His neighbor passes him the army man. Kathy smiles at Ian and says, brightly, "Great!"

Practical Positive Parenting

#7 Explain Why

What happens at this age is likely to shape future behaviors, which is why I love this commandment. It fosters an open conversation between parent and child that, with any luck, will persevere into the teenage years. This one goes to the heart of positive discipline: teaching your children the fact that their actions have effects on others and encouraging them to recalibrate their behavior of their own will.

Explaining why is simply providing your child with information that they may not actually have, or may not have connected to this situation. You'll be pleasantly surprised at the cooperativeness of a child who is armed with logical, simple information.

An important part of explaining the why is picking the right moment. Be sure to avoid moments in which your child is very stressed, hungry, or otherwise dealing with external effects. Try to use examples from your child's past to help them understand the current situation. If they have lived it, they'll be that much more able to understand.

In Real Life…

Your child is starting school and is ready for more responsibility, like picking up his toys after he plays with them. He has his Legos all spread out across the floor. After about fifteen minutes, he gets tired of them and gets up and runs into the other room. You call him back and ask him to clean up, but he says "No!" and runs out of the room again. You follow him into the other room and ask him to sit down. You ask him again to clean up his toys, and he says simply that he doesn't want to. You decide to explain why it is important. "You know how when mommy is cooking, she uses the green bowl, right?" you ask. Your son nods. "Well, what would happen if mommy didn't wash the bowl after she finished cooking?" Your son thinks. "We wouldn't have a bowl for the popcorn on movie night," he says.

Practical Positive Parenting

"That's right," you say. "And that would mean…"

"No popcorn!" he says. You can see the light bulb going on.

"So do you understand why it's important to clean up after yourself?" you ask. He nods and silently walks into the other room to pick up his toys.

Practical Positive Parenting

#8 Try A Behavior Management System

Using a behavior management system is a great option for kids this age. What is a behavior management system? It may sound complicated, but it really just means any systematic way of teaching good behavior, with a clear goal, reward and consequence set in place. A behavior management system essentially gamifies good behavior, making it fun for the child to comply, and rewarding good behavior.

You've probably heard of different behavior management systems—there are plenty to choose from. Some parents use tokens, which are part of kits that are sold and used to globally manage chores and behavior. An easy one that you can do with what you have on hand is the docking system. If your child is old enough to get an allowance, you can set guidelines and rules for behavior that include taking a small portion of the allowance every time there is a transgression. Or, you can start with a zero allowance and add money for desired behavior. These rewards-based models of behavior management are excellent tools to promote good behavior with kids this age.

In Real Life…

Haley's children are always begging and cajoling her for more screen time. Todd, 5, and Lisa, 6, each have their own iPad. Haley has put the parent protections on it, so she knows they are watching mostly wholesome stuff. However, she wants to limit the time they spend on it. It feels like every day they are pushing and testing the waters, trying to get more and more time on their screens. Haley feels like she is constantly having to fight them to pay attention to her and follow the rules. One day, instead of threatening to take away their iPads, she pulls out the kitchen timer. She sets it to thirty minutes and explains to the two children that when the timer beeps, screen time is over and the iPads should be returned to their chargers. She explains the consequence if this is not accomplished. Then she leaves the room. The timer starts its backward count.

Practical Positive Parenting

When the timer goes off, thirty minutes later, she watches as the kids both get up, put the iPads in their place and go off to play and do their homework. She can't believe how well it worked, but she supposes it's a lot harder to argue with a machine than with her!

Practical Positive Parenting

#9 Set Time To Connect

Creating time to connect with your little one fosters a sense of love and caring between you and your child. When we schedule time to be alone with our children, they get a big message: they are important enough to make demands on our time. Nothing says 'I love you' like spending your time with your child, engaged and completely focused on them.

Time set aside one-on-one with your child often results in insight into their lives and any challenges they may be going through. Just by virtue of having nothing "scheduled," spontaneous conversation flourishes, and children are really fun to have spontaneous conversations with. A bonus? You are laying the foundation here for a healthy relationship with your slightly-less-open and charming future teenager.

I recommend booking this time into your calendar as you would an appointment or a work meeting. Make it non-negotiable. Because, after all, is there really anything more important you have to do?

In Real Life…

You notice your little one is acting out more than usual. It's been a busy month, with lots of school activities and family commitments, and looking back you realize that you haven't had much time together with her. You set aside two hours on a Thursday afternoon to be with her, and instead of making plans or scheduling something productive to do with her, you just leave those two hours wide open. When the time comes, the two of you plop down on the sofa and just stare at each other. She starts to giggle, and you do too. Before you know it, she is telling you about her day at school in more detail than she ever has, and you even find out which boy has been chasing her around the playground. None of this would have happened without this special block of time.

Practical Positive Parenting

#10 Encourage Independent Problem Solving

Of all the commandments, this one is probably the most global and amorphous. It is a constant, something that you will have to work on making a shift for if you don't already practice it, but it is the most likely to equip your little one for future successes. Teaching your child independent problem solving is important because it teaches them that they are capable, and that they have agency in their lives. This helps to raise responsible, resourceful children.

To encourage independent problem solving in your child, there are a few key actions you should keep in mind.

First, don't jump in too soon when you see your child in a mild predicament. Allow them to work through the problem and any negative feelings that it arouses, as long as it is safe for them to do so.

Secondly, if you say no to something and your child doesn't accept it, instead of always being unilateral and stuck on the original no, remain a bit open to your child's petition. If your child can present their side and use logic and charm to present a solution that meets both of your needs, you can accept their negotiation and explain why you did. Far from backtracking, this makes your child feel powerful, listened to and teaches them the art of compromise.

In Real Life...

Vanessa is at the park with her son Bryan. She is watching him play with a few other children on the playground. One of the other boys takes his toy and Bryan hits him. Vanessa runs over, separates the children, and takes Bryan to sit with her.

"You're angry because that boy took your toy," she says. "I would be, too, but you can't hit him." Bryan stares angrily past Vanessa. "What could you do instead?" she asks.

Bryan kicks at the dirt. "Take it back from him!" he says.

"Well that's a start," says Vanessa. "You could also ask him to give you the toy, couldn't you?"

"But he wouldn't!" says Bryan.

"You don't know until you try," says Vanessa. "If he didn't, what could you do then?"

Bryan thinks. "Come and get you?" he says.

"Great idea!" says Vanessa. "You know hitting is not allowed, so next time this happens, remember to find another way. Now how can we make this better right now?"

"I'll say I'm sorry," says Bryan.

~ 11 ~

CONCLUSION: YOU'RE ON YOUR WAY

It has been an honor accompanying you on your journey toward positive parenting. I hope that this book, full of theory and practice on how to incorporate positive parenting into your life, has been both interesting and useful.

The extra effort in positive parenting is really, at its most basic, tuning in and staying close to your child, transmitting love to them every chance you get. If you follow the steps and the calls to action, you will see changes in your child's behavior over time. With you as a guide, your children will grow into the most amazing adults!

Keep this book around to consult every now and then. As your child grows, new challenges will crop up and sections that didn't seem relevant once may help guide you through a rough spot.

Practical Positive Parenting

I strongly encourage you, on the journey toward positive parenting, to savor each and every success and bit of progress that you have. And remember, success is relative! What for one parent may be a daily occurrence (an easy bedtime, for example) might be a BIG win for you. And that's okay. Take the extra step to jot these successes down in a journal, and that way you can look back at them when you're feeling like progress is too slow.

Above all, relax. Spending time with your kids and watching them grow into wonderful people is what parenting is all about—so enjoy the journey!

YOU CAN CHANGE MY LIFE

I hope this book has given you value. I'm positive that if you follow what I've written, you will be on your way to creating that positive connection and truly bonding with your child. You can change your child's life through positive parenting.

I have a tiny favor to ask. If you liked the book, would you mind taking a minute to write your feedback on Amazon about it? I check all my reviews and love to get feedback (that's the real reward for the months of work that went into writing this book—knowing that I'm helping people).

Use the link or QR code below to leave a review on Amazon.com

Use the link or QR code below to leave a review on Amazon.co.uk

Now, I don't just want to sell you a book—I want to see you put the advice outlined in this book into action.

As you work toward your goals, however, you'll probably have questions or may run into some difficulties. I'd like to be able to help you with these! I answer questions from readers every day.

Here's how we can connect:

Practical Positive Parenting

Email: Hannah@AtmosPublishing.com

Keep in mind I get a lot of emails every day, and answer everything personally, so if you can keep yours as brief as possible, it helps me ensure everyone gets helped!

Also, if you have any friends or family who might enjoy this book, spread the love, and lend it to them!

Or do better!

Email them and me in the same email and **I'll send them the eBook or paperback version for free!**

Thanks again and I wish you the best!

Hannah

P.S.

If you didn't like the book, please send me an email with your comments. I take all constructive criticism seriously and will do my best to improve the book.

Practical Positive Parenting

HANNAH'S OTHER BOOKS & NEW RELEASES

Sign up to be the first to know about Hannah's new books and get early copies as well as audiobooks **for free** using the link or QR code below.

https://bit.ly/2FIV4hF

References

[i] Gottman, J., Goleman, D., & Declaire, J. (2011). *Raising An Emotionally Intelligent Child.* (pp. 42–68). New York, United States: Simon & Schuster.

[ii] Positive Psychology Center. (2020). Retrieved April 18, 2020, from https://ppc.sas.upenn.edu

[iii] Seligman, M. (2011). *Authentic Happiness.* Amsterdam, Netherlands: Amsterdam University Press.

[iv] Lonczak, H. (n.d.). Positive Psychology. Retrieved April 19, 2020, from https://positivepsychology.com/positive-parenting/

[v] Gottman, John, and Joan DeClaire. *Raising an Emotionally Intelligent Child.* New York, NY: Simon & Schuster, 1998. Print.

[vi] Positive parenting can have lasting impact for generations. (2017, October 5). Retrieved April 24, 2020, from https://today.oregonstate.edu/archives/2009/sep/positive-parenting-can-have-lasting-impact-generations

[vii] Phelan, T. (2016). *1-2-3 Magic* (Sixth Edition). Naperville, IL: Sourcebooks.

[viii] Chapman, G., & Campbell, R. (1997). *The 5 Love Languages of Children: The Secret to Loving Children Effectively* (3rd ed.). Chicago, IL: Northfield Publishing.

[ix] About Positive Discipline. (2020, February 20). Retrieved May 9, 2020, from https://www.positivediscipline.com/about-positive-discipline

[x] Somayeh, G., SayyedMirshah, J., & SayyedMostafa, S. (2013). Investigating the Effect of Positive Discipline on the Learning Process and its Achieving Strategies with Focusing on the Students' Abilities. *International Journal of Academic Research in Business and Social Sciences, 3*(5), 306–312. Retrieved from http://hrmars.com/admin/pics/1894.pdf

[xi] Siegel, D. J., & Bryson, T. P. (2014). *No-Drama Discipline.* New York, NY: Bantam Books.

[xii] Markham, L. (2015). *Peaceful Parent, Happy Siblings*. Zaltbommel, Netherlands: Van Haren Publishing.

Made in the USA
Middletown, DE
29 August 2020